Furigana JAPAN

Everything You Should Know about the Life of Modern Japan Q&A

Abe Naobumi
Michael Brase = translator

げんだいにほん
現代日本の
く
暮らしQ＆A

あ べ なお ぶみ
安部直文
やく
マイケル・ブレーズ＝訳

Furigana JAPAN
現代日本の暮らし Q&A
Everything You Should Know
about the Life of Modern Japan Q&A

© 2017 IBC Publishing, Inc.

Published by IBC Publishing, Inc.
Ryoshu Kagurazaka Bldg. 9F, 29-3 Nakazato-cho
Shinjuku-ku, Tokyo 162-0804, Japan

www.ibcpub.co.jp

All rights reserved. No part of this book may be reproduced in
any form without written permission from the publisher.

First edition 2017

ISBN978-4-7946-0478-1

Printed in Japan

About *Furigana JAPAN*

Reading Sets You Free

The difficulty of reading Japanese is perhaps the greatest obstacle to the speedy mastery of the language. A highly motivated English speaker who wants to make rapid progress in a major European language such as Spanish, French or German need only acquire a grasp of the grammar and a smattering of vocabulary to become able to at least attempt to read a book. Thanks to a common alphabet, they can instantly identify every word on the page, locate them in a dictionary, and figure out—more or less—what is going on.

With Japanese, however, *kanji* ideograms make it infinitely harder to make the jump from reading with guidance from a teacher to reading freely by oneself. The chasm dividing the short example sentences of textbooks from the more intellectually rewarding world of real-world books and articles can appear unbridgeable. Japanese—to borrow Nassim Taleb's phrase—is an "Extremistan" language. *Either* you master two thousand *kanji* characters with their various readings to achieve breakthrough reading proficiency and the capacity for self-study *or* you fail to memorize enough *kanji*, your morale collapses, and you retire, tired of floating in a limbo of semi-literacy. At a certain point, Japanese is all or nothing, win or lose, put up or shut up.

The benefits of staying the course and acquiring the ability to read independently are, of course, enormous.

Firstly, acquiring the ability to study by yourself without needing a teacher increases the absolute number of hours that you can study from "classroom time only" to "as long as you want." If there is any truth to the theories about 10,000 hours of practise being needed to master any skill, then clearly the ability to log more hours of Japanese self-study has got to be a major competitive advantage.

Secondly, exposure to longer texts means that your Japanese

input rises in simple quantitative terms. More Japanese *going into* your head means that, necessarily, more Japanese *stays in* your head! As well as retaining more words and idioms, you will also start to develop greater mental stamina. You will get accustomed to digesting Japanese in real-life "adult" portions rather than the child-sized portions you were used to in the classroom.

Thirdly, reading will help you develop tolerance for complexity as you start using context to help you figure things out for yourself. When reading a book, the process goes something like this: You read a sentence; should you fail to understand it first time, you read it again. Should it still not make sense to you, you can go onto the next sentence and use the meaning of that one to "reverse-engineer" the meaning of its predecessor, and so on. By doing this, you will become self-reliant, pragmatic and—this is significant—able to put up with gaps in your understanding without panicking, because you know they are only temporary. You will morph into a woodsman of language, able to live off the land, however it may be.

That is the main purpose of *Furigana JAPAN*: to propel you across the chasm that separates those who read Japanese from those who cannot.

Furigana the Equalizer

Bilingual books have been popular in Japan since the 1990s. Over time, they have grown more sophisticated, adding features like comprehensive page-by-page glossaries, illustrations and online audio. What makes the *Furigana JAPAN* series—a relative latecomer to the scene—special?

The clue is in the name. This is the first ever series of bilingual books to include *furigana* superscript above every single *kanji* word in the text. Commonly used in children's books in Japan, *furigana* is a tried-and-tested, non-intrusive and efficient way to learn to read *kanji* ideograms. By enabling you to decipher every word immediately, *furigana* helps you grasp the meaning of whole passages faster without needing to get bogged down in fruitless and demoralizing searches for the pronunciation of individual words.

By providing you with the pronunciation, *furigana* also enables you to commit new words to memory right away (since we remember more by sound than by appearance), as well as giving you the wherewithal to look them up, should you want to go beyond the single usage example on the facing English page. *Furigana JAPAN* provides a mini-glossary at the foot of each page to help you identify and commit to memory the most important words and phrases.

Raw Materials for Conversation

So much for *furigana*—now for the "Japan" part of the name. The books in this series are all about Japan, from its customs, traditions and cuisine to its history, politics and economy. Providing essential insights into what makes the Japanese and their society tick, every book can help you as you transition from ignorant outsider to informed insider. The information the books contain gives you a treasure trove of raw materials you can use in conversations with Japanese people. Whether you want to amaze your interlocutors with your knowledge of Japanese religion, impress your work colleagues with your mastery of party-seating etiquette and correct bowing angles, or enjoy a heated discussion of the relative merits of arranged marriages versus love marriages, *Furigana JAPAN* is very much the gift that keeps on giving.

We are confident that this series will help everyone—from students to businesspeople and diplomats to tourists—start reading Japanese painlessly while also learning about Japanese culture. Enjoy!

Tom Christian
Editor-in-Chief
Furigana JAPAN Series

まえがき

日本人って、どんな民族なの？
和食の特徴は？
いわゆる、裸祭りや命がけの奇祭とはどんなものなのか？
一番人気のお土産は何か？
最も人気のある温泉地はどこか？
日本が最近直面している問題とは何か？

上にあげたのは、日本についてよく聞かれる事柄の一例ですが、もっと多くのことが本書の中で説明されています。読者のみなさまが日本という国や日本人について、それも過去から現代に至るまで、多くのことを理解できることでしょう。日本はこれまでもよく、文化的にガラパゴス諸島であるとたとえられてきました。世界中の国々とはかけ離れ、独自の方向で文化的な進化を遂げてきたのです。しかし、そういった文化の発展がいまの日本のバックボーンを形作り、人々の関心を引き寄せているのです。たとえば、武道や生花などは世界的に注目されています。現代の日本はいまもなお文化的な革新を続けており、マンガ、アニメ、温かい便座など数多くの文化を生み出しています。

今の日本は、過去と現代が複雑に絡み合い、解読するのは必ずしも容易ではありません。本書は日本の全貌を、できるだけシンプルにみなさまに理解していただけるようにつくられました。観光客として来日するときでも、椅子に座って日本のことを空想するときにでも、是非、楽しんでください！

マイケル・ブレーズ

Introduction

What kind of people are the Japanese?
What is Japanese cuisine (*washoku*)?
What are the so-called naked and life-risking "bizarre" festivals?
What are the most popular souvenirs?
Which are the most famous hot springs?
What modern-day problems is Japan facing?

These questions, and many more, will be answered in this book, providing you with a greater appreciation for the country and its people, both modern and historical. Historically, Japan has often been a kind of cultural Galápagos, cut off from the rest of the world and evolving in its own unique direction. The culture developed then still forms the backbone of modern Japan and is well-worth being acquainted with, especially given the global spread of Japanese martial arts, flower arranging, and much more. Modern Japan has continued this tradition of cultural innovation, producing manga, anime, and heated toilet seats, to mention only a few.

Present-day Japan is an intricate mixture of the modern and the traditional, a convoluted complication that is not always easy to decipher. This book, as simple as it is, will help you enjoy Japan to the fullest, whether as a visiting tourist or as an armchair traveler. Enjoy!

Michael Brase

目次
もくじ

まえがき 6

第1章 暮らし

1 日本人の特質
Q: 日本人って、どんな民族なの？ 18
Q: イエス、ノーをはっきり言わないのは、なぜ？ 20
Q: 日本人の特性とは？ 22

2 衣
Q: 和服はどんな時に着るの？ 24
Q: 男性の和服の正装は？ 24
Q: 女性の和服の正装は？ 26

3 食
Q: 和食の特徴は 26
Q: 日本人の一般的な食事習慣は？ 28
Q: よく食べる魚料理にはどんなものがあるの？ 30
Q: 醤油・味噌はいつから使うようになったの？ 32
Q: うどん、そばの違いは？ 32
Q: 寿司はいつから食べるようになったの？ 34
Q: うなぎはいつから食べるようになったの？ 36
Q: 改まった席で出される料理とは？ 38
Q: 食器の正しい置き方は？ 40
Q: 日本酒の種類は？ 42
Q: 日本酒の飲み方は？ 44

4 住
Q: 日本の住宅の特徴は？ 46

Contents

Introduction 7

Chapter 1 Everyday Life

1 What Characterizes the Japanese People?
Q: What kind of people are the Japanese? 19
Q: Why can't Japanese give a clear yes or no answer? 21
Q: What are the outstanding Japanese cultural traits? 23

2 Clothing
Q: When is Japanese clothing worn? 25
Q: What does formal Japanese wear for men consist of? 25
Q: What does formal attire for women consist of? 27

3 Food
Q: What is Japanese cuisine (*washoku*)? 27
Q: What is the usual meal like? 29
Q: How is fish most often eaten? 31
Q: When did soy sauce and miso come to be used? 33
Q: What is the difference between udon and soba? 33
Q: When did sushi come into being? 35
Q: When did grilled eel become a favorite food? 37
Q: What is the most formal Japanese cuisine? 39
Q: Is there a fixed order to the placement of tableware? 41
Q: How many different kinds of saké are there? 43
Q: Is there a particular way to drink saké? 45

4 Japanese Housing
Q: What distinguishes Japanese housing? 47

Q: 土地や建物の値段はどのように決めるの？ 46
Q: 賃貸住宅の契約時にいくら必要？ 48
Q: 寝具の特徴は？ 48
Q: なぜ、玄関で靴を脱ぐの？ 50
Q: 畳は、なにでできているの？ 50
Q: 床の間って、なに？ 52
Q: 襖と障子の違いは？ 52

5　冠婚葬祭
Q: 子どもが産まれてすぐしなければならないことは？ 54
Q: 七五三とは、どんな行事なの？ 54
Q: 成人式とは、どんな儀式なの？ 56
Q: 日本人の一般的な結婚式とは？ 58
Q: 結婚式の費用はいくらかかるの？ 58
Q: 結婚のお祝いの相場は、いくら？ 60
Q: 日本人の結婚年齢は、いくつ？ 60
Q: 外国人との国際結婚は多いのですか？ 62
Q: 毎年、離婚する人はどれくらいいるの？ 62
Q: 日本人が祝う記念日にはどんなものがあるの？ 64
Q: 贈り物で注意しなければならないことは？ 66
Q: 日本の一般的な葬儀は？ 66
Q: 仏式の葬儀はどのように行われるの？ 68
Q: 葬儀の費用はいくらぐらいかかるの？ 68
Q: 埋葬はどのようにするの？ 70

6　行　事
Q: 国民の祝日は？ 70
Q: お正月は、なにをするの？ 76
Q: 節分って、どんな行事なの？ 76

Q: How is the price of land and houses decided? 47
Q: What is the initial cost of renting a house or apartment? 49
Q: What does Japanese bedding consist of? 49
Q: Why are shoes removed in the entryway? 51
Q: What are tatami mats made of? 51
Q: What is a *tokonoma*? 53
Q: What is the difference between a *fusuma* and a *shoji*? 53

5 Weddings and Other Special Occasions

Q: What is required after the birth of a child? 55
Q: What does 7-5-3 mean? 55
Q: What is the coming-of-age ceremony? 57
Q: What is a typical Japanese wedding? 59
Q: How much does a wedding cost? 59
Q: What is the going rate for a wedding gift? 61
Q: What is the average marriage age? 61
Q: Are international marriages common? 63
Q: How many divorces are there a year? 63
Q: What ages are objects of special commemoration? 65
Q: Is caution required in presenting a gift? 67
Q: What is the typical funeral like? 67
Q: What does a Buddhist funeral consist of? 69
Q: How much does a funeral cost? 69
Q: How are the deceased interred? 71

6 Holidays and Special Occasions

Q: What are the national holidays? 71
Q: What do people do on New Year's Day? 77
Q: What is *setsubun*? 77

Q: お彼岸とは？ …………………………………………… 78
Q: お節句とは？ …………………………………………… 78
Q: 七夕って、どんな日なの？ …………………………… 80
Q: お盆とは？ ……………………………………………… 80
Q: お月見って、なに？ …………………………………… 80
Q: 大晦日には、なにをするの？ ………………………… 82
Q: 他に、どんな行事があるの？ ………………………… 82

第2章　宗教

Q: 日本人は無宗教の人が多いの？ ……………………… 84
Q: 神道は、日本の国教なの？ …………………………… 86
Q: 靖国神社とは？ ………………………………………… 88
Q: 神社はお寺とどこが違うの？ ………………………… 88
Q: 神社参拝は、どのように行うの？ …………………… 90
Q: 仏教には、どんな宗派があるの？ …………………… 92
Q: 禅とは、どんな教えなの？ …………………………… 92
Q: 僧侶は、なぜ髪を剃っているの？ …………………… 94
Q: お寺での参拝の作法は？ ……………………………… 94

第3章　文化

1　学芸

Q: 日本人のノーベル賞受賞者は？ ……………………… 96
Q: 文化勲章とは？ ………………………………………… 98
Q: 日本の代表的なマンガ家・アニメ作家は？ ………… 98
Q: 世界的に有名な映画監督は？ ………………………… 100
Q: 世界で評価が高い音楽家は？ ………………………… 102
Q: 日本画は西洋の絵とどう違うの？ …………………… 104

Q: What is *higan*? 79
Q: What are *osekku*? 79
Q: What is Tanabata? 81
Q: What is Obon? 81
Q: What does "moon viewing" mean? 81
Q: What is *omisoka*? 83
Q: What other special events are there? 83

Chapter 2 Religion

Q: Why do so many Japanese say they are not religious? 85
Q: Is Shinto the state religion of Japan? 87
Q: What is the significance of Yasukuni Shrine? 89
Q: What makes a Shinto shrine different from a Buddhist temple? ... 89
Q: What is the proper procedure for praying at a Shinto shrine? 91
Q: How many Buddhist sects are there? 93
Q: What is Zen Buddhism? 93
Q: Why do Buddhist monks shave their heads? 95
Q: What is the proper procedure for praying at a Buddhist temple? .. 95

Chapter 3 Culture

1 Arts and Sciences

Q: How many Japanese have won the Nobel Prize? 97
Q: What is the Order of Culture? 99
Q: Who are the most famous Japanese manga and anime artists? ... 99
Q: Who is the most famous Japanese film director? 101
Q: Who are Japan's most acclaimed world musicians? 103
Q: What is the difference between Japanese painting and Western painting? 105

2 伝統技芸

- Q: 歌舞伎はいつから始まったの？ ……………………… 106
- Q: 歌舞伎はどこでやっているの？ ……………………… 108
- Q: 能と狂言はどんな関係なの？ ………………………… 108
- Q: 文楽とはどんな芸能なの？ …………………………… 110
- Q: 落語と講談の違いは？ ………………………………… 110
- Q: 生け花って、なに？ …………………………………… 112
- Q: 日本人は誰でも茶道の心得があるの？ ……………… 112
- Q: 家元制度って、なに？ ………………………………… 114
- Q: 陶磁器と漆器の違いは？ ……………………………… 114

- Q: 日本刀の特徴は？ ……………………………………… 116
- Q: 人間国宝って、なに？ ………………………………… 118
- Q: 大相撲はいつから始まったの？ ……………………… 118
- Q: 大相撲はいつ、どこでやっているの？ ……………… 118
- Q: 力士になるには？ ……………………………………… 120
- Q: 柔道と空手の違いは？ ………………………………… 120
- Q: 剣道の勝負はどうつけるの？ ………………………… 122
- Q: アーチェリーと弓道の違いは？ ……………………… 124

- Q: 囲碁、将棋のプロ棋士とは？ ………………………… 124
- Q: 競技かるたは、どんなゲームなの？ ………………… 126

3 現代の文化の特徴

- Q: 今の日本文化の特徴は？ ……………………………… 128
- Q: 日本人はコメを食べなくなったの？ ………………… 130
- Q: コンビニはいくつあるの？ …………………………… 130
- Q: スマホって、なに？ …………………………………… 132

2 Traditional Theater and Handicrafts

Q: What are the roots of the Kabuki theater? 107
Q: Where is Kabuki performed? 109
Q: What is the relationship between Noh and Kyogen? 109
Q: What is Bunraku? 111
Q: What is the difference between Rakugo and Kodan? 111
Q: What is ikebana? 113
Q: Is every Japanese familiar with the principles of the Way of Tea? 113
Q: What is the *iemoto* system? 115
Q: What is the difference between ceramic ware and lacquer ware? 115
Q: What are the outstanding characteristics of a Japanese sword? 117
Q: What is a Living National Treasure? 119
Q: When was the first sumo bout? 119
Q: When and where are sumo tournaments held? 119
Q: What are the requirements for becoming a sumo wrestler? 121
Q: What is the difference between judo and karate? 121
Q: How is the winner decided in *kendo*? 123
Q: What is the difference between Japanese archery (*kyudo*) and Western archery? 125
Q: What does it take to become a professional go or shogi player? 125
Q: What is competitive *karuta*? 127

3 Modern-day Culture

Q: What are the features of Japanese culture today? 129
Q: Is rice no longer eaten? 131
Q: How many convenience stores are there? 131
Q: What is a *sumaho*? 133

第4章　レジャー

- Q: 日本人の余暇の過ごし方は？ ………… 134
- Q: 海外旅行で人気がある国は？ ………… 136
- Q: 日本独特のレジャー施設は？ ………… 136
- Q: ゲームや漫画に熱中する大人がいるって、ほんとう？ …… 138
- Q: カラオケはいつからブームになったの？ ………… 140
- Q: パチンコはどんな遊技なの？ ………… 140

第5章　観光・イベント

1　観光

- Q: 日本への観光客が多い国は？ ………… 142
- Q: 外国人に人気がある観光地は？ ………… 144
- Q: 宿泊施設にはどんなものがあるの？ ………… 146
- Q: 世界遺産に登録されているのは、どこ？ ………… 146
- Q: 温泉って、なに？ ………… 150
- Q: 有名な温泉地は、どこ？ ………… 150
- Q: 日本のおみやげで人気があるのは？ ………… 154
- Q: 国宝って、どのように決めるの？ ………… 156
- Q: 仏像にはどんな種類があるの？ ………… 158
- Q: お城は、いくつあるの？ ………… 160

2　イベント

- Q: 有名な祭りは？ ………… 160
- Q: 祭りは、なんのためにやるの？ ………… 162
- Q: 花火大会は、いつから始まったの？ ………… 164
- Q: 灯篭流しって、なに？ ………… 164
- Q: かまくらって、なに？ ………… 166

Chapter 4 Leisure

Q: How do Japanese spend their free time?........................ *135*

Q: What are the most popular destinations for foreign travel?· *137*

Q: Are there any uniquely Japanese leisure facilities? *137*

Q: Is it true that mature adults are just as enthusiastic about comics and video games as young people?..................... *139*

Q: When did karaoke begin to boom? *141*

Q: What is pachinko? *141*

Chapter 5 Tourism and Special Events

1 Tourism

Q: What countries send the most visitors to Japan? *143*

Q: What are the most popular tourist sites?....................... *145*

Q: What kinds of accommodations are there for tourists?.... *147*

Q: How many World Heritage Sites are there? *147*

Q: What distinguishes Japanese hot springs?..................... *151*

Q: Which hot spring areas are the most well-known? *151*

Q What are the most popular souvenirs? *155*

Q: How is a National Treasure designated? *157*

Q: What kinds of Buddhist sculpture are there?.................. *159*

Q: How many castles are there?....................................... *161*

2 Special Events

Q: What are the most famous festivals? *161*

Q: What is the purpose of a festival?................................. *163*

Q: When did fireworks displays first begin? *165*

Q: What is lantern floating? *165*

Q: What is a *kamakura*? *167*

第1章
暮らし

富士山と茶畑（静岡県）Mt. Fuji and green tea fields, Shizuoka

1　日本人の特質

Q: 日本人って、どんな民族なの？

　世界の民族的な特徴は、狩猟民族と農耕民族に大別されます。狩猟民族は移動をして食料を得る必要があるため、狩りのテクニックや情報量がものを言います。一方、農耕民族は定住をして収穫の時を待つというタイプです。その意味で日本人は元来、農耕民族と言えます。
　特に稲作が定着した3世紀頃には、人口が250万ほどに増大し、大規模集落が各地に形成されました。稲の栽培はとても手間がかかり、田植えや稲刈りでは多くの人手が必要です。そこで勤勉と協調性が日本人の基本的な労働観として形成されたのです。この労働観が、戦後日本の経済成長の原動力になりました。

☐ 民族　people
☐ 大別される　be basically divided into
☐ ものを言う　to be effective
☐ 元来　basically
☐ 手間がかかる　labor-intensive
☐ 人手　hands of people

Chapter 1
Everyday Life

1 What Characterizes the Japanese People?

Q: What kind of people are the Japanese?

Peoples throughout the world can be basically divided into hunters and farmers. Hunters must be constantly on the move to gain sustenance, and they not only become adept at the techniques for stalking their prey but knowledgeable in the ways of their movements. Farmers, on the other hand, are sedentary and patient as they wait for harvest time. For the most part, Japanese belong to the farming or agricultural type.

By the 3rd century AD, when rice cultivation had become firmly established, the population had grown to about 2,500,000, and large-scale villages appeared throughout the country. The cultivation of rice was labor-intensive, with the planting and harvesting requiring the hands of many people. Cooperation and diligence were essential, and these characteristics became ingrained in the Japanese people. It was this work ethic that provided the driving force behind the rapid growth of the postwar Japanese economy.

第1章　暮らし

世界は今、高度情報化時代。これを主導したのは米国に象徴される狩猟民族です。どこにどんな獲物がいるかという情報量が貧富を分けるため、情報に対する意識が高いのです。欧米型の暮らしになじんできたことで近年、日本人の労働観も変質しつつあります。

Q: イエス、ノーをはっきり言わないのは、なぜ？

日本人は、外国人に比べて自己主張をしないと言われます。国際会議などで、「顔が見えない日本人」と揶揄されることもあります。要するに個性的でなく、何を考えているのか分からないというわけです。イエス、ノーをはっきり言わないのは、対人関係を悪くしたくないという思いが強いからです。これは、農耕民族として協調性が重視されてきたことと無縁ではありません。

「出る杭は打たれる」という言葉があるように、集団生活を維持するには皆が同じレベルであることが必要で、そこからはみ出す人は異端とされます。島国で狭い土地に住む日本人にとって、所属する集団の中で生きてゆくには、自己主張をしない、目立とうとしないことが大事な処世術なのです。

- □ 主導する　lead
- □ 貧富を分ける　make difference between rich and poor
- □ 意識が高い　immensely eager to
- □ 〜しつつある　began to
- □ 要するに　in short
- □ 思いが強い　concern
- □ 無縁ではない　undoubtedly have its roots
- □ はみ出す　stick out
- □ 異端　heretic
- □ 処世術　worldly wisdom

The world now has entered an information-intensive age. It has been led by hunter societies such as the United States. Since it is all-important to know the whereabouts of the prey, these societies are immensely eager to accumulate information. As Japan has become more and more familiar with Western ways, its work ethic has begun to undergo a gradual change.

Q: Why can't Japanese give a clear yes or no answer?

It is often said that Japanese are less assertive than other people. At international conferences and other such forums, Japanese have been described as being faceless, that they don't stand out as individuals, and that it is hard to know what they are really thinking. Japanese often don't give a clear-cut yes or no answer for fear of antagonizing the other party. This characteristic undoubtedly has its roots in the cooperation and collaboration that is so essential to an agricultural society.

As expressed in the proverb "The protruding nail is driven down," it is necessary for everyone to be on the same plane in order to sustain life in a communal setting; anyone who sticks out from the crowd is treated as a heretic. For Japanese, living in tightly-knit communities on small confined islands, getting along amicably with others means not being self-assertive and not drawing attention.

第1章 暮らし

Q: 日本人の特性とは？

　日本を訪れた外国人が驚くのは、一般的に日本人が礼儀正しく、清潔好きで、細やかな気配りをしてくれることだそうです。こうしたことも、農耕民族としての集団生活を通して**培われてきた特性**と言えるでしょう。

　日本は、外国と比べ四季の区別がはっきりしています。そして、**季節の移り変わり**を感じながら生活をしてきました。農耕民族には、自然を畏れながらも**共生する**知恵があります。外国人、特に欧米人を驚かせるもう一つが、神様が多いことです。これは、自然を神として**畏れ崇めてきたからに他なりません**。

　古来、日本は多神教の国です。一神教では神に**見放されたら救いはない**といった厳格性がありますが、多神教の日本では「捨てる神あれば、拾う神あり」という**ことわざ**が示すように、神と人間の関係はおおらかでゆるやかです。**とかく、ものごとをあいまいにしがち**な日本人の特性は、多神教の民族だったことも影響しているのです。

□ 培われる　be cultivated
□ 移り変わり　seasonal changes
□ 共生する　live in coexistence
□ 畏れ崇める　fear and revere
□ 〜に他ならない　none other than
□ 見放される　lose someone's favor
□ 救いはない　be beyond all help
□ ことわざ　proverb
□ とかく〜しがちだ　have a tendency to
□ ものごとをあいまいにする　leave things up in the air

Q: What are the outstanding Japanese cultural traits?

Foreign visitors to Japan often say they are surprised by how polite Japanese are, how cleanly, and how attentive to the smallest detail. These traits can be attributed to the communal life of an agricultural people.

Compared to many other countries, the four seasons of the year are very distinctive in Japan. The Japanese have long lived with these seasonal changes, observing and feeling them in their daily lives. Over time, Japanese developed the practical intelligence to live in coexistence with nature while at the same time fearing it. Another thing noted by foreign visitors, Westerners in particular, is the plethora of gods in Japan. This too is attributable to a long history of both fearing and revering nature.

Japan has been a polytheistic country from ancient times. In monotheistic countries, God is very strict, and once you have lost his favor, it is lost forever. But in polytheistic Japan, the relationship between the gods and man is much more flexible and forgiving, as indicated by the proverb "If one god disowns you, there is always another to save you." The Japanese tendency to leave things up in the air may have its origins here.

2　衣

Q: 和服はどんな時に着るの？

年配者や仕事上で着る必要がある人以外、日常的に和服を着る人はほとんどいなくなりました。年の初めに**気分を改める**ために和服で正月を迎えたり、仕事初めに女性が着物で出勤するといった風習がまだ見られますが、あとは伝統行事や結婚式などの祝い事で和服姿が見られる程度です。

着物の一種の浴衣は、和風旅館に宿泊すると**おなじみ**ですが、**略式**なので公式の場には出られません。近頃、夏の花火大会で浴衣を着て**見物する**若者が増えているのは、ファッションの一種のようです。

Q: 男性の和服の正装は？

男性の場合の正装は、黒紋服です。これを着るのは**生涯**一度、結婚式の新郎になった時だけという人も少なくありません。しかも黒でなく、**きらびやかな**色紋服が流行しているので、本来の正装である黒紋服の出番は**少なくなる一方**です。

紋服とは、家系を表す紋章を入れた和服のことですが、自分の家紋を知らない人もたくさんいます。

- □ 気分を改める　renovate one's spirit
- □ おなじみ　familiar
- □ 略式　informal
- □ 見物する　watch
- □ 生涯　all one's life
- □ きらびやかな　gorgeous
- □ 少なくなる一方である　go on diminishing

2 Clothing

Q: When is Japanese clothing worn?

Except for older people and those whose work requires it, Japanese clothing has virtually disappeared from daily life. Sometimes you see women wearing kimonos on the first working day of the New Year or on New Year's Day to mark a fresh start in the coming year. Otherwise, the principal occasions are traditional events, weddings and other celebrations.

The light cotton kimono called a *yukata* is a familiar sight at Japanese inns, but it is strictly informal and not to be worn out in public. However, young people can be seen wearing *yukata* at summer fireworks as a sort of fashion statement.

Q: What does formal Japanese wear for men consist of?

Formal attire for men consists of black wear emblazoned with the family crest (*kuro-mon-puku*). For many men, the only occasion on which they wear such formal attire is on their wedding day. Recently more colorful formal wear with the family crest has become popular, and so the need for black formal attire is gradually diminishing.

While it is true that formal men's garb requires the family crest, many people these days don't know what their family crest is.

浴衣　*Yukata*

男性の和服の正装　黒紋服
Kuro-mon-puku, formal wear for men

第1章 暮らし

Q: 女性の和服の正装は？

女性の場合の正装は、**既婚者**は留袖、未婚者は振袖とされます。留袖は黒地に**家紋**を入れ、**膝下**には華やかな模様が描かれています。振袖は色地に**あでやかな**模様が描かれ、袖丈が足元近くまである大振袖、それよりも短い中振袖、小振袖があります。

外出用の**略式**の和服として訪問着があり、既婚・未婚を**問いません**。女性の和服には時と場所による決まりごとがあります。

未婚女性の和服の正装 振袖
Furisode, formal wear for unmarried women

3 食

Q: 和食の特徴は

日本人の食生活は、パンや肉類を多く食べる欧米型になってきています。2014年12月、ユネスコが「和食」を無形文化遺産に登録しました。その特長の一つに挙げられたのが栄養バランスに優れた食生活です。

□ 既婚者 married person　　□ あでやかな charming
□ 膝下 below the knees　　□ 略式 semiformal
□ 家紋 family crest　　□ 問わない do not matter

Q: What does formal attire for women consist of?

Formal wear for women is divided into two types: *tomesode* for married women and *furisode* for unmarried. *Tomesode* is a black kimono with a family crest and a colorful design on the area below the knees. The *furisode* has a colorful design on a colored background and sleeves of three different lengths (long, medium, and short), with the longest reaching the floor.

There are also semiformal kimonos for women, worn when going out and paying visits, in which there is no difference between married and unmarried women. According to time and occasion, there are numerous rules governing women's wear.

3 Food

Q: What is Japanese cuisine (*washoku*)?

While on the one hand Japanese are eating more Western food like meat and bread these days, on the other hand Japanese cuisine was named an Intangible Cultural Heritage by UNESCO in December 2014. One of the features of *washoku* was said to be its superlative nutritional balance.

和食の基本はコメを主にした一汁三菜で、ご飯に汁もの、おかず三種(主菜一品、副菜二品)で構成されたメニューです。動物性油脂が少ないことから肥満防止に役立ち、ご飯は栄養価が高いだけでなく腹もちが良いので、間食を避けることができます。しかし、日本ではコメ離れが進み、肉や菓子類など高カロリー食物を好む傾向が強くなり、肥満が社会問題化しています。ユネスコに申請する際の和食の定義は、「三世代前の日本人が家庭で常食としていたもの」だったそうです。和食は日本人にとって、過去の遺産的存在になりつつあります。

Q: 日本人の一般的な食事習慣は？

一日三食で、家族全員が揃って食べる家庭は少なくなりつつあります。朝食はパンや牛乳といった欧米型の食事が増え、昼食は昔は家庭で作った弁当を食べるのが一般的でしたが、今は学校給食や外食ですませてしまう人が大半です。サラリーマンや生徒達には朝食抜きが増えていることが指摘されています。夕食は比較的、家族全員が揃って食べることが多いようですが、それでも週に二、三日程度と言われます。

家庭の食事は、子供達の好みを反映するためハンバーグやカレーライスなどになりがちで、昔からの和食が敬遠される理由もここにあります。

□ 主菜　main dish
□ 副菜　side dish
□ 肥満防止　guard against obesity
□ 腹持ちが良い　filling
□ 間食　between-meal eating
□ 常食　customary meal
□ 〜ですませる　make do with
□ 抜き　skip
□ 敬遠する　give a wide berth

The traditional menu is described as *ichiju-sansai*, which means "one soup and three dishes." Basically, this indicates a meal composed of rice, a soup, one main dish, and two supplementary dishes. It is low in animal fat and thus a guard against obesity, and the rice is not only high in nutritive value but filling, warding off the desire to eat between meals. Of late, however, there is a strong tendency toward high-calorie foods such as meat and confectionaries, allowing obesity to raise its ugly head. When *washoku* was submitted to UNESCO for consideration, it was described as the customary meal in Japanese households three generations ago. For the Japanese people, it seems that *washoku* is slowly becoming a thing of the past.

Q: What is the usual meal like?

The number of families that eat three meals a day together is becoming rather rare. Breakfast consists simply of bread or toast and milk. Lunch, formerly a homemade box lunch, is now mostly a school cafeteria lunch or eaten out. Salaried workers and students often skip breakfast entirely. Dinner is when the family is most likely to come together, but even then it is often only two or three times a week.

Ichiju-sansai, "one soup and three dishes"

Even when the family sits down at the table together, the meal is most likely to consist of what the children favor, hamburger or curry rice. Traditional Japanese food is given a wide berth.

第1章 暮らし

Q: よく食べる魚料理にはどんなものがあるの？

外国人にもよく知られているのが、寿司、天ぷらです。**寿司ネタ**は魚介類の肉を薄く切ったものですが、寿司づくりは**習練**が必要なため専門店で食べるのが一般的です。

家庭でよく食べるのは魚介類の刺身で、ワサビやショウガと醤油をつけます。刺身の**定番**は、マグロです。

天ぷらにすると美味しいのがエビ、イカ、白身の魚などです。**揚げたて**を食べるのが、天ぷらの最も美味しい食べ方です。その他、**手軽**な調理法として、魚に塩をちょっと振りかけて焼く塩焼き、醤油をベースにした**タレ**を付けて焼く照り焼き、醤油の中に入れて煮込む煮付けなどがあります。

□ 寿司ネタ　sushi topping　　　　□ 揚げたての　freshly fried
□ 習練　practice　　　　　　　　□ 手軽な　simple
□ 定番　standard　　　　　　　　□ タレ　sauce

Q: How is fish most often eaten?

Abroad, the most widely known Japanese ways of eating fish are sushi and tempura. Sushi makes use of thinly sliced fish or other seafoods, and since the slicing is a rather delicate task, sushi is most often eaten out at a sushi restaurant.

At home, seafood fare consists mostly of fish (*sashimi*) and other seafood that has been sliced into eatable portions, dipped in ginger, *wasabi* mustard, or soy sauce. The standard for *sashimi* is tuna.

The seafoods most often used in tempura are shrimp, squid, and light meat fish. Tempura tastes best when it is still hot. Other simple ways of eating fish include grilling after lightly salting (*shioyaki*), grilling after applying a soy-based sauce (*teriyaki*), and stewing in soy sauce (*nitsuke*).

刺身
Sashimi

天ぷら
Tempura

第1章 暮らし

Q: 醤油・味噌はいつから使うようになったの？

　食材を微生物の働きで**発酵**させる方法は、人類が**太古の昔**に発見しました。日本では縄文時代の遺跡から、発酵食品をつくっていたことが確認されています。

　醤油も味噌も、その**原型**とされるものは8世紀頃からあったようですが、**庶民**の間で普及するようになったのは16世紀中頃と言われます。**いずれも**大豆を発酵させた調味料ですが、醤油は今や世界100か国で流通する日本を代表するブランド名になっています。

　大豆の発酵食品として、豆腐や納豆があります。豆腐は奈良時代に中国から日本に伝わったとされます。大豆は「畑の肉」と呼ばれるように、植物性たんぱく質が豊富で、肉や牛乳などのタンパク質に比べて脂肪分が少ないため、低カロリー食材として日本人が好んで食べます。しかし、原料の大豆の90％ほどを輸入に**頼って**います。

　その他の発酵食品には日本酒、茶、鰹節、漬物、寿司などがあります。

Q: うどん、そばの違いは？

　歴史的には、うどんは中国から伝わった**製法**をもとにした麺、そばは日本**独自**の麺という違いがあります。材料の違いは、うどんが小麦粉、そばがそば粉を使うことです。ただし、そばも**つなぎ**（接着材）に小麦粉を使っています。つなぎの小麦粉の割合や、卵や芋をつなぎとして使うことで、そばにはいくつかの種類があります。

□ 発酵　fermentation　　　　□ 庶民　common people
□ 太古の昔　primeval time　　□ いずれも　both
□ 原型　prototype　　　　　　□ 頼る　depend on

Q: When did soy sauce and miso come to be used?

Early humankind soon discovered how to prepare food by fermentation using microorganisms. In Japan, evidence of fermented foods has been discovered in sites from the Jomon period (about 12,000 to 300 BC).

Evidence of what might be called the prototypes of miso and soy sauce have been found from the 8th century, but it was only in the mid 16th century that they became widely used among the common people. Both are made from fermented soy beans and are now used as a representative Japanese seasoning in more than 100 countries around the world.

Natto and tofu are also made from fermenting soy beans. *Natto* is said to have been brought to Japan from China in the Nara period (710-784). Soy beans are so rich in vegetable proteins that they have been called the "meat of the fields." They are also low in fat compared to meat and milk, and have long been a favorite low-calorie food among Japanese. The beans themselves are mostly imported, accounting for nearly 90% of Japanese consumption.

Other fermented Japanese foods include saké, tea, *katsuobushi* (dried, fermented, and smoked skipjack tuna), pickled vegetables, and sushi.

Q: What is the difference between udon and soba?

Historically, udon are a type of noodles made according to a process that originated in China, while soba are noodles made in a uniquely Japanese way. As far as ingredients are concerned, udon is made of wheat flour, and soba of buckwheat. Soba also uses wheat flour as a binding. According to the ratio of wheat, and whether egg or yam is also used as a binding, there are various varieties of soba.

☐ 製法　process
☐ 独自の　unique
☐ つなぎ　binding

第1章 暮らし

また、醤油をベースにしたつゆの中に麺を入れ温めて食べる「かけそば」、冷たいつゆにつけて食べる「もりそば」など、食べ方もさまざまです。日本そばは、寿司・天ぷらと並ぶ代表的な日本料理とされます。

Q: 寿司はいつから食べるようになったの？

寿司の語源は「酸し」で、すっぱいことを意味していたというのが有力な説です。奈良時代頃から食べられていたようで、握り寿司などで使う酢飯に、そのなごりがあります。

昔は魚介類を飯と塩で乳酸発酵した「なれずし」が主流で、保存食として重宝されました。今も日本各地に、特有のなれずしが伝わっています。江戸時代になって、酢飯の上に魚介ネタを乗せて握って客に出す「早ずし」が流行し、これが現在の握り寿司（江戸前寿司）に受け継がれています。

❑ 江戸前寿司

江戸前とは、江戸の町の前に広がる海（現在の東京湾）にちなんだ言葉です。海では魚介類がたくさん獲れ、それを新鮮なうちに客にたべさせようと"早ずし"が工夫されました。

□ 〜と並ぶ along with
□ すっぱい sour
□ なごり trace
□ 重宝される be much valued
□ 受け継がれる come down
□ 工夫する invent

There are also differences in how soba is eaten depending on whether it is dipped in a warm soy-based sauce (*kakesoba*) or a cold sauce (*morisoba*). Along with sushi and tempura, soba is one of Japan's most typical foods.

Q: When did sushi come into being?

The etymological origin of "sushi" is probably the word meaning "sour" (*su*). Vinegared rice has been eaten since the Nara period (710-784), and the origin of the word has survived in the "sour" vinegared rice (*sumeshi*) used in *nigirizushi* (hand-pressed sushi).

In the distant past, the principal type of sushi was *narezushi*, which consisted of lacto-fermented seafoods and rice that was much valued as a way of preserving food. Even now local varieties of *narezushi* have come down to us. In the Edo period (1703-1868) a type of "quick" sushi became popular that featured seafood placed on vinegared rice and pressed conveniently together by hand. The present-day version of this is the familiar *nigirizushi* (or *Edomae-zushi*) that is so common today.

❏ *Edomae-zushi*

Edomae originally referred to the bay that was in "front of the town of Edo" (now Tokyo). The seafood caught in this bay (present Tokyo Bay) was delivered to customers while still fresh in the newly invented form of "quick sushi" or *Edomae-zushi*.

江戸前寿司
Edomae-zushi

Q: うなぎはいつから食べるようになったの？

　日本人の**好物**のうなぎは、古代人も食べていたようです。奈良時代にはむなぎと呼んでいたことが『万葉集』に記されています。栄養価が高く、体力増強にも役立つということで、日本では**夏バテ**防止のために**土用の丑の日**に食べると良いと言われていますが、これは江戸時代からの風習です。

　うなぎの調理法は、関東と関西で大きく異なります。関東では背中から切り分けるのですが、関西では腹から切り分けます。武士が多かった江戸では切腹に**通じる**として、うなぎの腹に包丁をあてるのを嫌ったためと言われています。

　2014年、ニホンウナギがIUCNレッドリストに絶滅危惧種として選定されました。日本人が食べるうなぎはほとんどが**養殖**もので、輸入うなぎも増えています。

- □ 好物　favorite food
- □ 夏バテ　summer doldrums
- □ 土用の丑の日　Midsummer Day of the Ox (according to ancient Chinese calendar system)
- □ 通じる　associate
- □ 養殖(の)　cultured

Q: When did grilled eel become a favorite food?

Eel was a favorite food of Japanese even in the distant past, and is mentioned in the Nara-period poetry anthology *Collection of Myriad Leaves* in the 8th century. High in nutritional value and said to be a fortifier against the summer doldrums, grilled eel has been especially recommended on the Midsummer Day of the Ox since the Edo period.

The preparation of eel differs greatly between the Kansai and Kanto regions. In Kansai, the eel is first sliced through the belly, but in Kanto this is done through the back. Since Kanto and Edo were the home of the samurai, they associated any reference to cutting the belly with ritual disembowelment (*hara-kiri* or *seppuku*), a subject they preferred not to contemplate. Or so the story goes.

In 2014 the Japanese eel was placed on the International Union for the Conservation of Nature and Natural Resources' list of threatened species. The eel eaten by Japanese today is mostly of the cultured variety, with imports increasing.

うな重
Unaju, grilled eel on rice

第1章 暮らし

Q: 改まった席で出される料理とは？

　結婚披露宴や料亭・旅館などで出される日本料理は、会席膳とも言います。この**献立**は一汁三菜(吸い物・刺身・焼き物・煮物)を基本としています。

　料理は①先付(前菜)、②椀物(吸い物)、③向付(刺身)、④鉢肴(焼き物)、⑤強肴(煮物)、⑥止め肴(酢の物またはあえ物)、⑦食事(ご飯・味噌汁・漬物)、⑧水菓子(果物)の順に出されます。

　同じ呼びかたの懐石は、**禅宗**の修行僧の食事に**由来**し、ルーツは同じなのですが、会席のほうは**酒席**で出される料理という大きな違いがあります。

□ 改まった席　formal place
□ 献立　menu
□ 禅宗　Zen ascetics
□ 由来する　originate
□ 酒席　banquet

Q: What is the most formal Japanese cuisine?

The cuisine served at weddings, high-class Japanese restaurants, and inns is called *kaiseki*, or simply put, dinner cuisine. It consists of the "one soup and three dishes" mentioned above (basically, soup, *sashimi*, something grilled, and something stewed).

The order in which dishes are served is as follows: 1) an appetizer, 2) clear soup, 3) *sashimi*, 4) grilled fish, 5) a dressed or vinegared dish, 6) something stewed, 7) the main course (rice, miso soup, and pickled vegetables), and 8) fruit.

There is another type of cuisine called *kaiseki* (though written with different Chinese characters), which originated in the food eaten by Zen ascetics. Though the two types of *kaiseki* have the same roots, the one mentioned in the previous paragraph is distinguished by the fact that it is served at banquets.

会席膳
Kaiseki-zen, formal Japanese cuisine

Q: 食器の正しい置き方は？

食事内容が欧米型になったと言っても、日本人が伝統的に行なってきた食事作法は、まだ受け継がれています。箸は頭を右にして手前に置く、ご飯茶碗は左、味噌汁は右に置くのが基本とされます。

箸の持ち方、使い方の作法もあり、正しい持ち方を子供の頃からしつける家庭も多く、料理を突き刺したり、皿の上であれこれと選ぶしぐさなどは禁じられています。

● 箸の正しい持ち方　The right way to hold chopsticks

① 箸の一本を、親指の腹と薬指の先で固定させる。

One chopstick is secured between the ball of the thumb and the tip of the ring finger.

② もう一本を、親指の先と中指の先で挟むようにして、上から人差し指を添える。

The other is held between the tip of the thumb and tip of the middle finger, and steadied by the index finger above.

③ 食べ物をつまむ時は、人指し指と中指を上下させる

Move the middle and index fingers up and down to pick up food.

□ 作法　etiquette
□ 手前に　in the forefront
□ しつける　teach someone manners
□ あれこれと　this or that
□ しぐさ　behavior

Q: Is there a fixed order to the placement of tableware?

Even while it is true that Japanese eating habits have become Westernized, traditional etiquette is still generally followed. The rule is for chopsticks to be placed in the forefront with the pointed end facing left, and the rice bowl on the left and soup bowl on the right.

The usage of chopsticks is also subject to various rules, with the right way to hold them taught to children in most households from an early age. Stabbing food or playing with it while deciding what to eat next is a definite no-no.

● お椀の開け方　The correct placement of bowls

蓋が付いているお椀は、蓋が開けにくい場合が多いが、開けかたにはちょっとしたコツがある。

Some bowls have lids, and these can be difficult to remove. However, there is a knack to it.

お椀の口を指で内側に軽く押さえ付けながら、蓋の上部をつまんで回すと簡単に開く。

Press down lightly on the rim of the bowl with your fingers, then hold the top of the lid and twist. It will open easily.

Q: 日本酒の種類は？

日本酒は「清酒」とも呼ばれます。原料は米、米麹、水です。米を**精米**して洗い、**糠**を取り除き、適当な分量の水を吸収させた後、**水を切って**蒸し、麹と水を加えて20日間ほど発酵させ、圧搾機にかけて酒と酒粕に**分離**します。分離した酒の滓を取り除いたものが、清酒です。

精米とは、米粒を磨いて内部のたんぱく質や脂肪を**削り取る**ことですが、削り取る割合を「精米歩合」と言い、これが50％以下が大吟醸酒、60％以下が吟醸酒、70％以下が本醸造酒といった区別がされています。

また、原酒は製成後にアルコール1％以上の**加水調整**をしていないもの、生酒は製成後に**加熱処理**をしていないものなどの分類もあります。

清酒は毎年7月から翌年6月を製造年度として、この間に出荷されたものを新酒、製成後1年以上貯蔵されたものを古酒、3年以上貯蔵されたものを長期貯蔵酒と呼んでいます。

□ 精米する polish rice
□ 糠 bran
□ 水を切る drain water
□ 分離する separate
□ 滓 lees
□ 削り取る scrape off
□ 加水調整をする delute
□ 加熱処理をする pasteurize

Q: How many different kinds of saké are there?

Japanese saké is also called *Nihon-shu*, or more accurately *seishu*. The ingredients are rice, yeast (*koji*), and water. The rice is polished and washed, the bran removed, the rice soaked in water, the water removed and the rice steamed, water and yeast (*koji*) added and fermented for 20 days, then placed in a compressor and the bran and saké separated. The lees are then removed, the result being *seishu*.

By polishing the rice, the protein and fats in the rice grains can be removed, and the percentage of weight remaining after polishing is called the rice polishing ratio. Types of saké are classified according to this ratio. If it is below 50%, the resulting saké is called *daiginjo-shu*; if below 60%, *ginjo-shu*; and if below 70%, *honjozo-shu*.

There are other ways of classifying saké. *Genshu* has not been diluted more than 1% ADV. *Namazake* has not been pasteurized.

Seishu refers to saké produced each year from July to June of the following year. Saké shipped during this period is called *shinshu* (new saké), and that aged for over a year is called *koshu* (old saké). Saké aged for over three years is called *choki chozo-shu* (long-term storage saké).

Q: 日本酒の飲み方は？

大きく分けると、温めて飲むのと、冷えた状態で飲む2つの方法があります。冷やというのは、冷蔵庫で冷やしたものではなく、本来は**常温**のお酒のことです。

温める場合は、**温度**によって表現が変わります。30度前後はひなた燗、37度前後は人肌燗、40度前後はぬる燗、45度前後は上燗、50度前後は熱燗、55度前後はとびきり燗などと言います。

こうした言葉の中に、繊細な日本人の感性と表現力の豊かさを**読み取る**ことができます。お酒を注文する時、「人肌燗で」などと言えば、**通人**です。

- □ 大きく分ける broadly classify
- □ 常温の at room temperature
- □ 温度によって according to the temperature
- □ 燗 warmed sake
- □ 読み取る gain an appreciation
- □ 通人 connoisseur

Q: Is there a particular way to drink saké?

Basically, there are two ways to drink saké, either hot or cold. "Cold" means at room temperature, not refrigerated.

Different terms apply when drinking saké hot, according to the temperature. Around 30 degrees is called *hinatakan* (sun-warmed), about 37 degrees *hitohadakan* (skin warm), about 40 degrees *nurukan* (lukewarm), about 45 degrees *jokan* (prime warmth), about 50 degrees *atsukan* (hot), and about 55 degrees *tobikirikan* (over-the-top hot).

Even in the names given to the temperatures of saké, one can gain an appreciation of Japanese sensitivity to the minutest matters. When ordering saké, if you casually say, "Make it *hitohadakan*," you will surely be considered a connoisseur.

日本酒 *Saké*

4 住

Q: 日本の住宅の特徴は？

日本の住宅は古来、木造でした。一方、西洋の住宅は伝統的に石造りです。ここに、日本人と西洋人の自然の捉え方の違いを見ることができます。石造りの住宅は堅牢で外界に対して閉鎖的ですが、木造住宅は開放的で、例えば中庭のように自然を積極的に取り込むといった工夫がされています。また、建材も天然素材を用いるのが和風建築の大きな特徴です。

しかし、1970年代以降、住宅の工業化が進むにつれて国産材の供給難や伝統工法を身に付けた職人の減少などで和風建築は衰退しつつあります。

Q: 土地や建物の値段はどのように決めるの？

土地・建物の面積は、日本独特の坪という単位で示します。一坪は、約3.3平方mです。土地の値段は法律で基準が決められ、それに基づいた実勢価格で取引されています。東京の都心部では、一坪数千万円という土地もあります。建物の値段は、使う材料のグレード次第ですが、坪単価50万円前後が一般的です。

例えば東京郊外で、都心まで1時間ほどの場所に約30坪（約100平方m）の一戸建て住宅を買おうとすると、3000～5000万円ほど必要になります。

- □ 古来　from the ancient past
- □ 堅牢　sturdy
- □ 外界　outside world
- □ 取り込む　incorporate
- □ 衰退する　go into a decline
- □ 実勢価格　realized price
- □ ～次第　depend on

4 Japanese Housing

Q: What distinguishes Japanese housing?

From the ancient past Japanese houses have consisted of wood. Western houses, on the other hand, have traditionally been made of stone. This difference allows a glimpse into how the two traditions view nature. Western housing is very solid and sturdy, creating a world of its own that holds nature at arm's length. Japanese housing, conversely, is open to nature and tries to incorporate natural elements into the house itself, such as seen in the creation of enclosed gardens that can be viewed from the interior. Another significant feature of Japanese housing is its use of architectural materials in their natural form.

However, in the 1970s the industrialization of housing construction began, domestic lumber was hard to come by, and experienced craftsmen became few and far between. The traditional wooden home went into a decline.

Q: How is the price of land and houses decided?

The area of land and houses (and buildings in general) is calculated in a unique Japanese measurement called a *tsubo*. One *tsubo* is the equivalent of 3.3 square meters. The price of land is decided on the basis of this legal standard. In central Tokyo one *tsubo* may cost as much as several tens of thousands of yen. The *tsubo* price of a building will be somewhere around ¥500,000, depending on the grade of the construction material.

If you want to buy a 30-*tsubo* (about 100 square meter) residence in the suburbs about an hour from downtown Tokyo, you could expect to pay ¥30-50 million.

Q: 賃貸住宅の契約時にいくら必要？

契約に際しては、①敷金（保証金）、②礼金、③仲介手数料、④1カ月分の家賃（入居日によって日割り計算）が必要です。敷金（通例は家賃の2カ月分）と礼金（同1カ月分）は家主が、仲介手数料（同1カ月分）は不動産業者が受け取ります。賃貸契約は一般的に2年契約で、続行する場合は更新料が必要になります。敷金は転居する際に返金されますが、室内を**破損**した場合などの修理費用は差し引かれます（東京の場合）。

Q: 寝具の特徴は？

日本伝統の寝具はふとんで、**体を横たえる**ための敷きぶとん、体の上に**かぶせる**掛けぶとんがあります。布の袋の中に綿が入っていますが、高級品には羊毛（敷きぶとん）や羽毛（掛けぶとん）を入れます。

ふとんには汚れ防止のカバーを掛けたり、シーツを敷き、これらを**取り換えて**使います。**寝汗**が**しみ込んだ**ふとんは、洗濯せずに**天日**で乾かします。ふとんは、使わない時は押入れなどに収納しておきます。

- 仲介　brokerage
- 破損する　damage
- 差し引かれる　be deducted
- 体を横たえる　lie
- かぶせる　cover
- 取り換える　change
- 寝汗　night sweat
- しみ込む　penetrate
- 天日　sunlight

Q: What is the initial cost of renting a house or apartment?

The initial costs upon signing a contract are 1) *shikikin* (security deposit), 2) *reikin* (key money), 3) *chukai tesuryo* (brokerage fee), and 4) the equivalent of one month's rent (paid pro rata depending on when occupancy takes place). The security deposit (usually equivalent to two-months rent) and the key money (also two months) are paid to the landlord; the brokerage fee is paid to the real estate agent. Contracts are generally for two years, and a renewal fee is required upon extension. The security deposit is returned when the renter moves out, but any fees paid for damage to the property are deducted, at least in the case of Tokyo.

Q: What does Japanese bedding consist of?

Traditional Japanese bedding consists of the futon (or *shikibuton*) for lying on and the *kakebuton* for covering oneself. The futon is essentially a bag with cotton inside, though pricier items contain wool (*shikibuton*) or down (*kakebuton*).

To keep them clean, futon have a cover or sheet, which are periodically changed. Futons that have accumulated some sweat are not washed but hung out in the sun. When not in used, futon are stored in a closet or elsewhere.

第1章 暮らし

Q: なぜ、玄関で靴を脱ぐの？

　外国人をしばしば戸惑わせるのが、家の玄関で靴を脱がなければならないことです。外観が洋風の家でも、玄関で靴を脱ぎスリッパにはき替えなければなりません。こうした習慣は、室内が畳の部屋だった時代のなごりが受け継がれていることによるものです。玄関から先は土足禁止…これが日本の流儀なのです。

Q: 畳は、なにでできているの？

　近頃は板張りの洋間が増えていますが、お年寄りほど畳敷きの和室を好む傾向があります。畳の表面は、イグサという植物を乾燥させて編み込んだ敷物でできています。板張りと違って柔らかく、独特の匂いがあり、心をなごませるのです。
　畳のサイズには地域性があり、関東の江戸間(880㎜×1760㎜)、関西の京間(955㎜×1910㎜)、団地間(850㎜×1700㎜)などがあります。畳は5年おき程度で、表面を新しいものに張り替えるのが良いとされます。

- □戸惑わせる　confuse
- □なごり　legacy
- □土足(で)　with one's shoes on
- □洋間　Western-style room
- □お年寄り　older people
- □編み込んだ　woven
- □心をなごませる　restful and relaxing
- □地域性　regionality
- □〜年おき　every 〜 years
- □張り替える　re-cover

Q: Why are shoes removed in the entryway?

One Japanese custom that sometimes confuses foreign visitors is the fact that shoes must be removed in the entryway. Even in homes that are Western in every other respect, shoes must be exchanged for slippers when entering the house. This custom is a legacy of the day when most of the rooms of the house were covered with easily soiled tatami matting. In any case, Japanese etiquette requires the shoes to be taken off before entering the house proper.

Q: What are tatami mats made of?

While Western-style rooms with wooden flooring are becoming ever more prevalent, older people still retain a liking for tatami-covered Japanese rooms. The surface of tatami consists of rush straw that has been dried and woven. Different from wooden flooring, tatami is soft and possesses a distinctive smell that is both restful and relaxing.

The size of one tatami mat varies somewhat according to region, with the Kanto size being 880 by 1760 mm, the Kansai size 955 by 1910 mm, and the *danchi* (apartment complex) size 850 by 1700 mm. It is generally held that every five years or so the surface of the tatami should be rewoven.

Q: 床の間って、なに？

家の中心的な和室の一画に作られた空間で、掛軸や生け花などを飾ります。床の間を背にした位置が上座で、客をもてなす時にはこの位置に座ってもらいます。

ちなみに、ビジネスマナーでもどこが上座なのかが重要視され、例えば応接室では入口から一番遠い座席が上座とされます。

Q: 襖と障子の違いは？

襖と障子は、いずれも和室の仕切り用の建具です。襖は、木の骨組みの両面に和紙や布を貼り、引き手が付いています。唐紙とも呼ばれることから、中国渡来のものと推察されます。

襖を日本独自に発展させたのが障子で、扉や窓としての役割があります。その歴史は古く、平安時代からとされます。木の枠に和紙を貼った障子は、電灯やガラスがなかった時代は採光のための建具として重宝されました。

また、一部がガラスで障子の部分を開閉できるものは「雪見障子」といって、部屋を閉めきったままで外の景色が見られます。このように風流を重視した点に、和風建築の特徴があるといっても過言ではありません。

- □ 一画　an area
- □ 〜を背にする　with one's back to
- □ もてなす　welcome
- □ 仕切り　partition
- □ 唐　Tang
- □ 〜渡来　come originally from
- □ 推察する　suspect
- □ 開閉できる　openable
- □ 締め切った　keep a door closed
- □ 重視する　weigh heavily
- □ 〜といっても過言ではない　It's not too much to say that

Q: What is a *tokonoma*?

The *tokonoma* is a recessed area built into the wall of the main Japanese room, where a hanging scroll or a flower arrangement is displayed. The primary guest or person at a gathering of people sits with his or her back to the *tokonoma*, a position known as the *kamiza* (superior seat).

The *kamiza* retains its importance in other venues, such as business meetings, where, for example, the seat nearest to the door of a reception room is consider the *kamiza*.

Q: What is the difference between a *fusuma* and a *shoji*?

Fusuma and *shoji* are both used as partitions in a Japanese room. A *fusuma* has a wooden frame covered with opaque Japanese paper (*washi*) or cloth on both sides and has a finger catch for opening and closing. From the fact that it is also called a *karakami* (Tang paper), it is suspected to have come originally from China.

The *shoji* is a Japanese enhancement of the *fusuma* and serves as a door or window. Its history is fairly old, with its first appearance being made in the Heian period (794-1185). The wooden frame is covered with translucent *washi*, which had the invaluable role of introducing sunlight into interiors in an age without electric lighting or glass.

In some later *shoji* the lower half is made of glass, over which the papered upper half can be raised or lowered. This is called a *yukimi shoji* (snow-viewing *shoji*), allowing the garden outside to be seen from the inside while keeping out the cold air. It is this integration of interior and exterior that forms one of the distinctive characteristics of traditional Japanese architecture.

5 冠婚葬祭

Q: 子どもが産まれてすぐしなければならないことは？

14日以内に、出生の届け出を市区町村役所にしなければなりません。「出生届書」は子どもの名前や両親についての必要事項を記載するほか、医師や助産師が記載する「出生証明書」が付いています。

したがって、子どもの名前は法律上、14日以内に決めなければならないのが原則です。子どもの名前を書いた「命名書き」を飾る習慣もあります。

また、生後100日目には、子どもの健康と成長を願って行う「お食い初め」という儀式も一般的に行なわれています。

Q: 七五三とは、どんな行事なの？

子どもの成長を願って、主に神社参拝をします。男の子は3歳と5歳、女の子は3歳と7歳になった年の11月15日に近所の神社に連れて行き、参拝後に「千歳飴」を食べる神事です。

江戸時代に始まったとされますが、地域によっては11月15日に限定していないケースもあります。

- □ 以内　within
- □ 届け出　notification
- □ 記載する　include
- □ 儀式　ritual
- □ 参拝する　visit to a temple [shrine]
- □ 神事　Shinto ritual
- □ ケース　case

5 Weddings and Other Special Occasions

Q: What is required after the birth of a child?

Within 14 days of the birth of a child, notification must be made to the nearest local government office. This birth registration includes not only the name of the child but pertinent information concerning the parents, as well as a birth certificate signed by the doctor or midwife in attendance.

Thus the name of the child must be legally decided within 14 days. There is also the custom of displaying in the home the name of the child written on a piece of special paper.

On the 100th day after birth, another ritual is commonly held called *okuizome* (first meal), in which the future health and well-being of the child is prayed for.

Q: What does 7-5-3 mean?

This refers to a visit to a temple or, more commonly, a shrine to celebrate the growth and well-being of young children. This takes place on November 15 when boys are three and five years old and when girls are three and seven. In conclusion, the children are given *chitose-ame* (thousand-year candy) to eat.

This custom is said to have started in the Edo period (1703-1868). According to the region, the day is not necessarily restricted to November 15.

千歳飴 *Chitose-ame*

第1章 暮らし

Q: 成人式とは、どんな儀式なの？

　子どもから大人になることを意味し、日本では**満20歳の男女**（前年の4月2日〜翌年4月1日の間）を招いて、毎年成人の日、またはその前日の日曜日に市区町村が主催して「成人式」が行われています。

　元来、日本では奈良時代以降から11〜16歳の**男児**が成人したことを示す儀式が行われ、**武士階級**の「元服」はよく知られています。成人を20歳としたのは明治時代からで、欧米にならったとされます。

　「成人式」では成人代表や**来賓**のスピーチなどが主で、出席者は記念品をもらって帰ります。参加者の多くは友人たちと再会できる場ということで、おしゃれをして出かけるチャンスと考えているようです。なかには、目立とうと奇抜な言動をして周囲の**ひんしゅくを買う**新成人もいて、警官隊が出動する会場もあります。

　ちなみに、2015年の新成人人口はおよそ126万人（男性65万人、女性61万人）で、21**年ぶりに**増加しました。

- □ 満〜歳　~ years old (counting by Western style)
- □ 男児　boy
- □ 武士階級　samurai class
- □ 来賓　invited guest
- □ ひんしゅくを買う　be frowned upon
- □ 〜年ぶりに　for the first time in ~ years

Q: What is the coming-of-age ceremony?

The coming-of-age ceremony is an annual rite of passage celebrating the transition from childhood to adulthood. Ceremonies are held by local administrative units for all twenty-year-olds (that is, those who have turned twenty between April 2 of the previous year and April 1 of the following year). It is a national holiday.

From the Nara period (710-784) onward, a coming-of-age ceremony was held for boys reaching adulthood between the ages 11 and 16. Among the samurai class, the rite of passage called *genpuku* is one example of this. In the Meiji period (1868-1912), twenty was designated as the age when adulthood is reached, supposedly following Western example.

The ceremony consists mainly of speeches by represent-atives of the new adults and the invited guests, after which the young participants receive commemorative gifts as the ceremony concludes. Most of the guests apparently look upon this occasion as an opportunity to meet old friends and dress up accordingly. Now and then, feeling their newly found independence, some of the new adults get a little out of hand, causing such fusses that the police is called for.

In 2015 the new adult population reached some 1,260,000 (650,000 men and 610,000 women), the largest number in 21 years.

第1章 暮らし

Q: 日本人の一般的な結婚式とは？

日本で広く行われているのが、神前結婚式です。特に信仰心がなくとも、神様の前で結婚の誓いをすることを、現代の若者はごく当たり前のこととして受け入れているようです。これはキリスト教の教会での挙式に憧れる女性が多いことにも共通しています。

結婚式場やホテルでは、祭壇を常設して神主や牧師に出張してもらうといった方法を採用しています。近年は、宗教色をなくした人前結婚式も普及し始めています。

結婚式は身内だけが出席し、記念撮影をした後、招待客が待つ宴会場に移動して新郎新婦のお披露目をします。

Q: 結婚式の費用はいくらかかるの？

招待客の数が、挙式費用の目安になります。結婚式場の場合は、一般的に招待客70名でおよそ350万円といったところが相場です。つまり、招待客一人当り5万円前後で予算を組む必要があります。そんなにお金がないという場合は、グレードを下げたり、招待客数を減らす、会場を変えるなどの工夫をしなければなりません。

結婚式は本人たちだけでなく、両家のプライドも関わってくるため、どうしても華美になりがちです。親に挙式費用の支援をしてもらった新婚夫婦は約7割とも言われます。一方で、たった一日のためにお金を使うのは嫌と、二人だけで記念写真を撮って終わりというケースも増えています。

□ 広く行われる be performed widely
□ ごく当たり前 quite common
□ 挙式 wedding ceremony
□ 宗教色 religious atmosphere
□ お披露目をする introduce
□ 目安 indication
□ 相場 standard fee
□ 両家 two families

Q: What is a typical Japanese wedding?

The most common type of wedding is a Shinto ceremony. Even though the happy couple may not be particularly religious, they have no qualms about pledging their troth before the Shinto gods. The same applies to marriages at Christian churches, which are especially fashionable among young women.

In wedding halls and large hotels, altars have often become permanent fixtures, and priests and ministers are invited to provide the services. In recent years civil services before family and friends are also on the increase.

The actual wedding ceremony takes place before close family only, followed by commemorative photographs. The bride and groom then repair to a spacious reception hall to greet relatives and friends assembled there.

Q: How much does a wedding cost?

The number of invited guests provides an indication of what the costs will be. The standard fee for 70 guests would be about ¥3,500,000, that is, about ¥50,000 per person. If this is prohibitive, then the overall quality of the ceremony must be ratcheted down a notch, the number of guests cut back, or a less expensive venue found.

Since it is not only the wishes of the bride and groom that are involved but the pride of the two families, weddings tend to be rather gorgeous. Weddings in which the families have chipped in to cover costs amount to some 70% of the whole. Still, some couples are reluctant to spend so much money on a single day of their lives, leading to the increasing incidence of weddings that end with the commemorative photograph.

☐ 華美　gorgeous
☐ 支援　cover

第1章 暮らし

Q: 結婚のお祝いの相場は、いくら？

披露宴に招待された場合、**お祝い金**をいくら**包む**べきか悩む場合が多いようです。お祝い金の額は**時代によって**変わってきていますが、友人や職場の同僚なら3万円、職場の**上司**や**目上**の親戚なら5万円、親族は5〜10万円というのが今の相場とされます。

Q: 日本人の結婚年齢は、いくつ？

昔は結婚年齢が低く、女性は10代で**嫁ぐ**のが当たり前とされた時代もありましたが、今は25〜34歳が多くなっています。2013年の人口動態調査では、初婚の女性約46.2万人のうち、25〜29歳が約19.4万人、30〜34歳が約10.9万人で、合わせると6割**強**を占めています。男性もほぼ同様の傾向が見られます。

□お祝い金 monetary gift　　□目上の superior
□包む enclose　　□嫁ぐ marry into
□時代によって with the times　　□強 more than

Q: What is the going rate for a wedding gift?

At Japanese weddings it is customary to present the bride and groom with a monetary gift rather than a present. The amount involved is often the subject of considerable cogitation. While it is true that this type of thing changes with the times, the standard now seems to be ¥30,000 for friends and colleagues, ¥50,000 for higher-ups at the workplace and older relatives, and ¥50,000 to ¥100,000 for close family.

Q: What is the average marriage age?

The marriage age used to be much lower than now. There were times, in fact, when it was entirely acceptable for women to marry in their teens, though now between 25 and 34 is becoming more common. The demographic survey for 2013 shows that out of about 462,000 women marrying for the first time, 194,000 were between 25 and 29, and about 109,000 were between 30 and 34, accounting for more than 60% of the total. The same trend is evident for men as well.

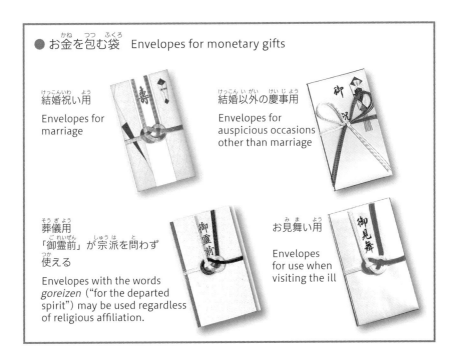

第1章 暮らし

Q: 外国人との国際結婚は多いのですか？

国際的な交流が進んでいる近年、国際結婚は増加しています。2012年の人口動態調査では年間の婚姻件数約75.7万組のうち、日本人男性と外国人女性のカップルが約1.7万組、日本人女性と外国人男性のカップルが約6500組でした。これは正式に届けを出した数なので、内縁関係のカップルを含めるともっと多くなります。

外国人の妻で多いのが中国人（約42％）とフィリピン人（約20％）、夫で多いのが韓国・朝鮮人（約28％）と米国人（約18％）です。

Q: 毎年、離婚する人はどれくらいいるの？

2013年の人口動態調査では、1年間の離婚件数は約23.1万件でした。2分16秒ごとに1組の夫婦が離婚をしたことになります。正式な離婚に至らないまでも、同居していながら会話もない家庭内離婚も増加しています。日本の法律では、離婚後6カ月以上たたなければ再婚できないことになっています。

□ 届けを出す　register with
□ 内縁関係　common law marriage
□ 〜ごとに　per
□ 〜に至らないまでも　have not yet led to
□ 〜していながら　in spite of

Q: Are international marriages common?

With the modern-day increase in international exchange, the frequency of international marriages has also increased. According to the demographic survey for 2012, of the 757,000 marriages that took place, those between a Japanese man and a foreign woman amounted to about 17,000, and marriages between a Japanese woman and a foreign man to about 6,500. This counts only marriages that have been registered with the authorities; if common law marriages were included, the numbers would be much higher.

Cases where the wife is Chinese account for about 42%, and where Filipino, about 20%. Among marriages where the husband is a foreigner, North and South Koreans account for about 28%, and citizens of the United States for about 18%.

Q: How many divorces are there a year?

According to the 2013 demographic survey, the number of divorces reached 231,000 a year. That means there was a divorce every 2 minutes 16 seconds. The number of couples who are living together but otherwise have no communication is also on the increase. Incidentally, Japanese law states that a woman cannot remarry until six months after the date of divorce.

Q: 日本人が祝う記念日にはどんなものがあるの？

一般的なものとしては「**長寿祝い**」があります。元来は奈良時代に中国の風習を取り入れたもので、**やがて**日本独自のものに発展しました。年齢の数え方は、昔は生まれた年を1歳として新年を迎えるごとに1歳ずつ加えた数え年を用いていましたが、今は**還暦**以外は満年齢で祝う人が多いようです。

還暦　（60歳）
古稀　（70歳）
喜寿　（77歳）
傘寿　（80歳）
米寿　（88歳）
卒寿　（90歳）
白寿　（99歳）
百寿・鶴寿　（100歳）

日本では、**かつて**100歳まで長生きする人は珍しかったのですが、今は5万人以上もいる長寿社会になっています。

他には、結婚25年目を祝う銀婚式、50年目を祝う金婚式などがあります。

□長寿　venerable age　　　　□還暦　sixtieth birthday
□やがて　gradually　　　　　□かつて　formerly

Q: What ages are objects of special commemoration?

The most common dates for celebration are those that have to do with reaching a certain venerable age. This custom was introduced from China in the Nara period (710-784) and gradually took on a unique Japanese form. Until the recent past the way ages were calculated was different from today. A new-born baby was considered one year old at birth and then gained another year with the coming of the New Year. This is called *kazoedoshi*. Now, except for *Kanreki* (celebrating the age of 60), most people count their age based on their birthday (this is called *mannenrei*). The principal days for celebrating old age are as follows:

Kanreiki   (60)
Koki   (70)
Kiju   (77)
Sanju   (80)
Beiju   (88)
Sotsuju   (90)
Hakuju   (99)
Hyakuju or Kakuju   (100)

Formerly, the number of people who reached the age of 100 was rather few, but now there are over 50,000.

Other days calling for celebration are the 25th year of marriage (the silver anniversary) and the 50th year (the gold anniversary).

第1章 暮らし

Q: 贈り物で注意しなければならないことは？

病気のお見舞いなどでは、鉢植えの花は「根付く＝寝付く」という意味で**縁起が悪い**とされているので避けなければなりません。同様に4（＝死）、9（＝苦）という数も**不吉**とされがちなので、果物などを贈り物にする場合は、数に**気を付ける**必要があります。

Q: 日本の一般的な葬儀は？

葬儀は宗教と**関連が深い**のですが、特定の信仰をしていない日本人の場合、仏式で葬儀をするのが一般的です。これは、江戸時代の国民すべてが寺に所属するという**檀家**制度のなごりが現在にも続いていることによるものです。

日本人の大半は、仏教寺院の墓地に**先祖代々**のお墓があります。そのため、亡くなった人を埋葬する関係上、**必然的**に仏式で葬儀をすることになるのです。

- □ 縁起が悪い of bad omen
- □ 不吉 unlucky
- □ 気を付ける give attention
- □ 関連が深い have a strong association
- □ 檀家 parishioner
- □ 先祖代々の ancestral
- □ 必然的 of necessity

Q: Is caution required in presenting a gift?

When taking a gift to someone in the hospital, potted plants are to be avoided because "taking root" is a homonym for "taking to bed." Likewise anything that has to do with the numbers 4 and 9 is considered unlucky because they are homonymous with "death" and "agony." When giving someone fruit or anything that is countable, care must be taken with how many there are.

Q: What is the typical funeral like?

Funerals usually have strong religious associations, but except for special cases, Buddhist funerals are the norm for most Japanese. This is a legacy of the Edo-period system according to which all Japanese had to be registered at a Buddhist temple.

The majority of Japanese have a family tomb at a Buddhist temple where their ancestors have been laid to rest. Consequently, when a funeral takes place, it is of necessity conducted according to Buddhist convention.

Q: 仏式の葬儀はどのように行われるの？

亡くなると、まず**通夜**が行われます。本来は遺族や近親者が終夜、遺体を見守ることを意味していましたが、現在は葬儀場などに遺体を運び、多くの参列者を迎えてお別れをしてもらう儀式になっています。そして翌日、故人の**成仏**を祈る葬式に引き続いて最後の別れを行う告別式が行われます。告別式の後、遺体は遺族や近親者が付き添って火葬場に運ばれ、火葬にされます。

仏教では死者の霊は49日間、**この世とあの世**の中間にとどまっているとされるため、亡くなった日を含め7日ごとに霊をなぐさめる法要を行うのが正式とされますが、現代では簡略化され、最初の7日目の「初七日」は葬儀の際に行い、最後の7日目の「四十九日」の法要だけ行うのが一般的です。

なお、遺族や近親者のみで通夜、葬式を行う場合を「密葬」と言います。

Q: 葬儀の費用はいくらぐらいかかるの？

全国平均で約200万円というデータがあります（日本消費者協会調べ、2010年）。これには、葬儀費用（平均約126万円）、寺院費用（平均約51万円）、飲食接待費用（平均約45万円）が含まれています。葬儀費用の最低額は20万円で、"密葬"の場合の費用のめやすになります。

- □ 通夜　wake
- □ 遺族　bereaved family
- □ 成仏　achieving Buddhahood
- □ この世とあの世　this world and the world to come
- □ とどまっている　be in a state of suspension
- □ なぐさめる　console
- □ 〜の際に　at the time of

Q: What does a Buddhist funeral consist of?

When someone passes from this life, the first rite to be held is a wake. This originally meant that blood relatives and close family would spend the entire night with the deceased. Now it generally means moving the body to a funeral home where large numbers of family and friends participate in a rite of final departure. The next day, after prayers are offered for the deceased's achieving Buddhahood, a ceremony of final farewell is held. The family and close relatives then accompany the deceased to a crematorium where the body is cremated.

According to Buddhist belief, since the spirit of the deceased is in a state of suspension between this world and the world to come for the first 49 days, every seven days a ceremony is held to console the departed spirit. In recent practice, this is generally abbreviated so that a service is held on the 7th day and then on the 49th.

Wakes and services attend by family alone are called *misso* (lit., cryptic services).

Q: How much does a funeral cost?

According to the Japan Consumers' Association (2010), the national average is ¥2,000,000. This includes funeral services (¥1,260,000), temple costs (¥510,000), and reception and refreshment fees (¥450,000). The minimum cost of funeral services is ¥200,000, which is the approximate cost of "cryptic" services.

Q: 埋葬はどのようにするの？

宗教に関係なく遺体は**ほとんどの場合**、火葬にされます。日本では昔は遺体をそのまま地中に埋める土葬も**多く見られ**ましたが、土地不足や衛生上の問題から土葬が制限されるようになりました。一部ですが、土葬を認めている**自治体**もあります。

火葬後の**遺骨**は**骨壺**というケースに入れ、しばらくの間、自宅で家族が**供養**・保管した後、お墓に**納め**ます（納骨）。

6 行事

Q: 国民の祝日は？

日本には1948年に制定された「国民の祝日に関する法律」があり、2014年6月の**法改正**で「山の日」（8月11日）が新たに加えられ、2016年から年間日数が16日となります。祝日が日曜日と重なるときは、翌日の月曜日は休みです。

- □ ほとんどの場合 in most cases
- □ 多く見られる be commonly practiced
- □ 自治体 local government body
- □ 遺骨 ashes of the deceased
- □ 骨壺 urn
- □ 供養する hold a memorial service
- □ 納める inter
- □ 法改正 law amendment

Q: How are the deceased interred?

Regardless of religious persuasion, cremation is the general rule. In the not too distant past, burial in the earth was commonly practiced, but with the increasing lack of sufficient space and due to hygienic reasons, this tradition came under restriction. Some—though not many—local government bodies still allow burial in the earth without cremation.

After cremation, the ashes of the deceased are placed in an urn and kept in the family home where they can be offered daily prayers. After an appropriate period has elapsed, the urn is interred in the family tomb.

6 Holidays and Special Occasions

Q: What are the national holidays?

The Public Holiday Law was established in 1948 and last amended in June of 2014, at which time Mountain Day (August 11) was added (to be first observed in 2016), bringing the total number of holidays to 16 for 2016. When a holiday overlaps with a Sunday, the following Monday becomes a holiday. The national holidays are as follows:

第1章 暮らし

- ▶ 元日（1月1日）
  年の初めを祝う。2日、3日を加えた3日間は**連休**になるのが一般的。

- ▶ 成人の日（1月の第2月曜日）
  20歳の人の祝い。

- ▶ 建国記念の日（政令で定める日 2月）
  2月11日に行われていた**紀元節**にちなむ祝日。国を愛する心を養う日と**意義付け**られているが、反対論もある。

- ▶ 春分の日（3月20日または21日）
  太陽が春分点を通過する日で、自然を**たたえ**、生物を**いつくしむ**日と定義されている。

- ▶ 昭和の日（4月29日）
  昭和天皇の生前、天皇誕生日として祝っていたのを継続した。2006年まで、みどりの日と呼ばれていた。

- ▶ 憲法記念日（5月3日）
  1947年のこの日に新憲法が施行されたのを記念する日。

- ▶ みどりの日（5月4日）
  3日と5日が祝日なので3連休にしようとの**意味合いが強い**のは、4月29日だったのをこの日に移動させたことからうかがえる。

- ▶ こどもの日（5月5日）
  こどもの健康、幸福を願う日。昔の男児の成長を祝う「端午の節句」にちなむ。

□ 連休 holidays in a row
□ 紀元節 Empire Day
□ ちなむ be connected with
□ 意義付ける define
□ たたえる celebrate
□ いつくしむ treat kindly
□ 意味合いが強い intended

- **New Year's Day (January 1)**
  To celebrate the beginning of the year. The 2nd and 3rd are traditionally added for a three-day holiday.

- **Coming of Age Day (second Monday in January)**
  To celebrate reaching the age of 20. See also "coming-of-age ceremony."

- **Foundation Day**
  (a day in February to be established by government ordinance)
  To celebrate the foundation of the nation and love of country. It replaces a prewar holiday known as *Kigen-setsu* (held on February 11) and has many detractors as a remnant of nationalism.

- **Vernal Equinox Day (March 20 or 21)**
  To celebrate nature and living things on the day when the sun crosses the vernal equinox.

- **Showa Day (April 29)**
  Originally to celebrate the birthday of Emperor Showa during his lifetime. Until 2006 it was known as Greenery Day.

- **Constitution Memorial Day (May 3)**
  To celebrate the day in 1947 when the postwar constitution went into effect.

- **Greenery Day (May 4)**
  To celebrate and commune with nature. By moving this day from April 29 to May 4, the intent was apparently to create three consecutive holidays in combination with May 3 and May 5.

- **Children's Day (May 5)**
  To celebrate the health and happiness of children. It takes place on the day that traditionally marked the growing-up of male children (*Tango no Sekku*).

第1章　暮らし

- ▶ 海の日（7月の第3月曜日）
  1941年に制定された海の記念日を復活させた祝日で、本来の7月20日に戻そうという声も高まっている。

- ▶ 山の日（8月11日）
  海の日があるなら山の日もつくろう、ということでできた祝日。八という漢字が山の形を連想させるので8月になったとの説もある。

- ▶ 敬老の日（9月の第3月曜日）
  老人を敬い、長寿を祝う日。1966年に制定された。

- ▶ 秋分の日（9月22日または23日）
  太陽が秋分点を通過する日。亡くなった人をしのぶ日ともされる。

- ▶ 体育の日（10月の第2月曜日）
  1964年に開催されたオリンピック東京大会を記念して66年に制定。99年までは10月10日だった。

- ▶ 文化の日（11月3日）
  日本国憲法が公布された1946年11月3日を記念して制定された祝日。

- ▶ 勤労感謝の日（11月23日）
  天皇家の新嘗祭という神事にちなんだもので、敗戦直後にGHQによって収穫祭とされた時期を経て1948年に制定された。

- ▶ 天皇誕生日（12月23日）
  今上（現在の）天皇の誕生日を祝う日。

□ 声が高まる　there is an argument　　□ 公布する　promulgate
□ 連想させる　resemble　　　　　　　□ 新嘗祭　Harvest Festival
□ しのぶ　remember　　　　　　　　　□ 今上　present

- **Marine Day (third Monday in July)**
  To celebrate the blessings of the ocean. It represents a rebirth of Marine Memorial Day established in 1941. Some argue that it should be returned to July 20, where it was originally.

- **Mountain Day (August 11)**
  The rationale for this day seems to have been, if there is a marine day there should also be a mountain day. According to some quarters, August was chosen because the shape of the Chinese character for 8 resembles a mountain (August is called the Eight Month in Japanese).

- **Respect for the Aged Day (third Monday in September)**
  To show respect for the elderly and celebrate long life. This day was established in 1966.

- **Autumnal Equinox Day (September 22 or 23)**
  To celebrate the day on which the sun crosses the autumnal equinox. It is also a day on which to honor one's ancestors and remember the dead.

- **Health and Sports Day (second Monday of October)**
  Originally established in 1966 to commemorate the opening of the Tokyo Olympics (1964). Until 1999 it was held on October 10.

- **Culture Day (November 3)**
  This day was established to commemorate the promulgation of the postwar constitution on November 3, 1946.

- **Labor Thanksgiving Day (November 23)**
  This day replaced an imperial Shinto rite called *Niiname-sai* and was established in 1948 after first being designated a harvest festival by the postwar occupation forces.

- **Emperor's Birthday (December 23)**
  To celebrate the birthday of the present emperor.

Q: お正月は、なにをするの？

年の初めに**あたる**正月は、本来は収穫を**つかさどる**神や、祖先の霊を迎える行事です。玄関の門松やしめ飾りは神々を迎えるためのもので、丸い鏡餅を**供える**のは神様に食べてもらうためです。

正月は家族が集まってお屠蘇というお酒を飲んだり、汁の中に餅を入れたお雑煮やお節料理を食べ、その後に神社や寺に出掛けて1年を健康で無事に過ごせるように祈ります。1日～3日の間の初詣で参拝者が多いベスト3（2014年）は、明治神宮（約316万人・東京都渋谷区）、成田山新勝寺（約305万人・千葉県成田市）、川崎大師（約302万人・神奈川県川崎市）。

Q: 節分って、どんな行事なの？

立春（2月3日または4日）の前日に、それぞれの家で行う「**邪気を払い、福を招く**」行事です。「鬼は外、福は内」と声を出しながら豆をまきます。大阪では節分に恵方巻と呼ばれる太巻き寿司を食べると**縁起が良い**、とされています。

- □ ～にあたる correspond to
- □ つかさどる govern
- □ 供える offer
- □ 邪気を払う purifying bad fortune
- □ 福を招く attract good fortune
- □ 縁起が良い bring good luck

Q: What do people do on New Year's Day?

In origin New Year's Day is a day on which the gods of the harvest and family ancestors are celebrated. The *kadomatsu* (lit., gate pines) and *shimenawa* (sacred straw cords) that decorate the front of houses are there to welcome the gods, and the *kagamimochi* (round rice cakes) set out are meant as a repast for the gods.

New Year's is a time for the family to come together and drink a special saké called *otoso*, eat a clear or white miso soup (*ozoni*) containing rice cakes, partake of a special meal of traditional New Year's food (*osechi-ryori*), and thereafter visit a temple or shrine to pray for health and happiness in the coming year. This "first visit" is called *hatsumode*. The three sites with the most visitors during the three-day New Year's period are 1) Meiji Shrine in Shibuya Ward, Tokyo (about 3,160,000), 2) Narita-san Shinsho-ji in Narita City, Chiba Prefecture (about 3,050,000), and 3) Kawasaki Daishi in Kawasaki City, Kanagawa Prefecture (about 3,020,000).

Q: What is *setsubun*?

Setsubun (lit., season division) is the last day of winter, which falls on February 3 or 4. It also refers to the "bean-scattering" ceremony that takes place on this day. In each household, beans are scattered as a way of purifying the house of bad fortune and attracting the good, while the words "Devils out, good fortune in" are shouted. In Osaka *futomaki-zushi* (thick sushi rolls) called *ehomaki* are eaten on this day to bring good luck.

Q: お彼岸とは？

彼岸とは仏教用語で「あの世」を意味します。先祖や亡くなった方の供養のためにお墓参りなどをします。お彼岸の期間は年2回で、春彼岸（3月の春分の日とその前後3日間の計7日間）と秋彼岸（9月の秋分の日とその前後3日間の計7日間）です。

Q: お節句とは？

子どもの成長を願って行う行事で、女の子は3月3日の「桃の節句」、男の子は5月5日の「端午の節句」があります。それぞれ平安時代、奈良時代から主に**貴族階級**が行った祝事にちなみます。女の子の家では雛祭りをし、男の子の場合は鯉のぼりを室外に立てます。

☐ 雛祭り

昔の衣装を着た雛人形を飾り、桃の花や白酒を**そえて**、女の子の成長を祝います。江戸時代から始まったとされます。

☐ 武者飾り

男の子の節句では、**強くたくましく**育ってほしいとの願いを込め、武士が着用した武具のミニュチュアや武者人形を室内に飾ります。

☐ 供養　memorial service　　　　☐ 貴族階級　noble class
☐ お墓参り　visiting a tomb　　　　☐ そえる　accompany
☐ 節句　seasonal festivity　　　　☐ 強くたくましく　strong and brave

Q: What is *higan*?

Literally meaning "the other shore," *higan* is a Buddhist term referring to the world of enlightenment. Visits are paid to the family tomb on this day to pray for one's ancestors and the recently deceased. *Higan* occurs twice a year, on the vernal and autumnal equinoxes, including the three days before and after.

Q: What are *osekku*?

Osekku (lit., seasonal festivity) refers to events carried out in the hope that one's children will grow up healthy and happy. The one for girls, *Momo no Sekku* (Peach Festival; also called Dolls' Day or Girls' Day), is held on March 3. The boys' festival, *Tango no Sekku* (Beginning Horse Festival; taken from the Chinese zodiac), is held on May 5. They trace their roots back to felicitous occasions in the Nara (710-784) and Heian (784-1185) periods. The girls' festival is highlighted by indoor displays of dolls dressed as Heian-period aristocrats, and the boy's by pennants in the shape of carp (*koi-nobori*) for flying outside.

❑ Dolls' Festival

These displays of dolls in period costumes, accompanied by peach blossoms and special white saké, are a means of invoking health and happiness. The present form is said to have originated in the Edo period (1603-1868).

❑ Armored Samurai

Another part of the Boys' Festival is the display of miniature armored samurai in the hope that the boys in the family will grow up strong and brave.

雛飾り (左)
武者飾り (右)

Hina kazari (l.)
Musha kazari (r.)

第1章 暮らし

Q: 七夕って、どんな日なの？

七夕は、7月7日の夜、天の川をはさんで**離ればなれ**の牽牛星と織女星が年1度会うという中国の伝説に由来した行事です。

この日は、**短冊**に願い事を書いて、竹の枝に結びつける**風習が伝**えられてきました。

Q: お盆とは？

お盆は、亡くなった親族や祖先の霊を供養する行事で、7月13日～16日（地域によっては8月13日～16日）の間に行われます。元来は仏教行事でしたが、宗教に**かかわらず**日本の伝統行事になっています。13日に迎え火をたいて霊を迎え入れ、16日に**送り火**をたいて霊をあの世に送り返します。

Q: お月見って、なに？

月を**鑑賞**する行事は、奈良時代以降に中国から伝えられたとされます。お月見の日は、だんご、もち、さといも、ススキを供えて月をながめます。1年で最も美しいとされる9月**中旬**の満月を、中秋の名月と言います。旧暦8月15日に当ることから十五夜とも呼ばれます。日本独自の行事として旧暦9月13日のお月見は十三夜と言い、だんごの他にクリや枝豆をお供えして鑑賞します。

- □ 離ればなれ　separated
- □ 短冊　strip of paper
- □ 風習が伝えられる　custom related to this day
- □ ～にかかわらず　regardless of
- □ 送り火　ceremonial bonfire
- □ 鑑賞する　appreciate
- □ 中旬　mid

Q: What is Tanabata?

The Tanabata (lit., the evening of the seventh) festival has its origins in the Chinese legend about a cow herd and a weaver princess who, separated by the Milky Way, can meet only once a year. It is held on the seventh day of the seventh month.

One custom related to this day is that of writing a wish on a special piece of paper and tying the paper to a bamboo branch.

Q: What is Obon?

Obon (from a Sanskrit word meaning "hanging upside down") refers to the custom of praying for ancestors and recently deceased from July 13 to 16, or (depending on the region) from August 13 to 16. Originally, Obon was a Buddhist practice but now it has become a pervasive part of Japanese culture. On the 13th fires are lit to welcome the returning spirits, and on the 16th fires are lit again to see them off to the other world.

Q: What does "moon viewing" mean?

The practice of viewing the moon as an object of aesthetic beauty is said to have been introduced to Japan from China in the Nara period (710-784). On that day various objects are put on display as offerings to the moon, such as rice dumplings (*dango*), rice cakes (*mochi*), eddoe (*satoimo*), and pampas grass (*susuki*). The moon is said to be most beautiful when full in mid September and is called the "wonderful moon of mid-autumn" (*chushu no meigetsu*). From the fact that it appears on August 15 on the old Japanese calendar, it is also called the "full-moon night of the 15th" (*jugoya*). In a particularly Japanese variation on this custom, September 13 on the old calendar is referred to as "the full-moon night of the 13th" (*jusanya*), when *dango*, chestnuts, and green soy beans (*edamame*) are displayed as offerings to the moon.

Q: 大晦日には、なにをするの？

　12月31日の大晦日は、1年の区切りをつける日です。家の大掃除、お正月の準備などで多忙な年末の最終日を家族揃って過ごし、除夜の鐘を聞き、元日の朝まで起きて新しい年神様を迎える年越しの行事が各地で行われます。

Q: 他に、どんな行事があるの？

　春は、お花見です。古くには梅の花を観賞するのがお花見とされたようですが、日本のお花見といえば桜が定番になっています。桜の花は、パッと咲いてパッと散ることから、武士道のいさぎよさに通じるとして愛でられたのです。

　桜は日本中で咲きますが、縦に長い列島ということで、南と北では時期が異なります。気象用語の桜前線は、北上する桜の開花日を示します。

　夏は、花火大会です。花火は江戸時代に隅田川で打ち上げられたのが始まりで、現在は全国各地で大規模な花火大会が開催されています。冬の花火大会もあります。

　秋は紅葉狩りといって、紅葉を鑑賞しに出掛ける人々がたくさんいます。日本人は、四季を楽しむためにさまざまな行事を生み出してきたのです。

- □ 区切りをつける　mark the end
- □ 多忙な　busy
- □ 除夜の鐘　bells on New Year's Eve
- □ 年越し　year-crossing
- □ 古くには　in the distant past
- □ パッと　quick to
- □ いさぎよさ　decisiveness
- □ 愛でる　admire
- □ 北上する　stretch from south to north
- □ 打ち上げる　set off

第1章　暮らし

Q: What is *omisoka*?

Omisoka refers to December 31 or New Year's Eve and is an important date in marking the end of one year and the beginning of the next. The family comes together as a whole, the house undergoes a year-end cleaning, and the bells of nearby Buddhist temples ring out at midnight to signify the washing-away of the illusions and delusions of the past year. People stay up till early morning to greet the gods of the new year, and various events take place in local areas throughout the country.

Q: What other special events are there?

First of all is the appreciation of the beauty of flowers, called *hanami* (lit., flower viewing). In the distant past this referred to the plum blossom, but now it is associated exclusively with the cherry blossom. Cherry blossoms are quick to bloom, and quick to scatter, and thus are thought analogous to the spirit of the samurai, who faced death without the least hesitation.

Since the Japanese archipelago stretches from south to north, the blooming of the cherry tree varies from region to region. The weather bureau uses the term cherry-blossom front (*sakura zensen*) to indicate this movement.

Summer is distinguished by its fireworks displays. The first of these displays is said to have taken place along the Sumida River in the Edo period (1603-1868), but now large-scale events can be seen throughout the country. There are even some that take place in winter.

In autumn there is *momijigari* (lit., maple hunting), and many people make excursions to view the changing of the leaves. This is just one of the many customs that involve an appreciation of seasonal changes.

第2章
宗教

伊勢神宮(三重県) Ise jingu, Mie

Q: 日本人は無宗教の人が多いの？

国内の宗教法人(約18万)の報告による信者数は、以下の通りです(2013年文化庁データ)。

```
神道系        約1億77万人
仏教系        約8470万人
キリスト教系   約192万人
諸教          約949万人
```

合計で2億人弱になります。人口が1.3億人弱なので人口よりも信者数が多いというわけです。なぜ、このようなことが起きるかというと、各宗教団体の報告のまま集計しているからです。

- □宗教法人 religious organization
- □以下の通り as below
- □諸 various
- □〜のまま conformable to

Chapter 2
Religion

Q: Why do so many Japanese say they are not religious?

There are approximately 180,000 religious organizations in Japan, with their number of adherents as listed below (2013, Ministry of Culture).

    Shinto linage   (about 100,770,000)
    Buddhist lineage   (about 84,700,000)
    Christian lineage (about 1,920,000)
    Others   (about 9,490,000)

    The total comes out to a little less than 200,000,000, which is odd since the population of Japan is only around 130,000,000. The reason for this discrepancy is that the total has been calculated on figures provided by the religious organizations themselves.

ところで、日本人に「あなたが信じている宗教は何ですか？」と尋ねると、「ありません」と答える人が多いはずです。ところが「あなたの家の宗派は何ですか？」という質問には、「**たしか、浄土宗だったような気がする**」といった返答が多くなります。

たしかに無宗教を**公言**する人が多いのは事実ですが、先祖代々、何らかの宗教に関わってきたというのが日本人なのです。特に仏教系は江戸時代にはどこかの寺院に所属しなければならないとされ、神道系は明治時代以降の国家神道の定着で国民総信者となった歴史があります。上記のデータはそれを反映したもので、個人の信仰の**対象**としてでなく、先祖が所属していたなごりなのです。

Q: 神道は、日本の国教なの？

神道は日本固有の宗教ですが、明治維新後に天皇を神格化する国家神道になりました。太平洋戦争の敗戦で**政教分離**が行われ、その後は数多い宗教の一つになっています。敗戦直後、**神を祀る**神社は全国に約11万ありましたが、そのほとんどが宗教法人として**現在に至って**います。

□ 宗派 sect
□ たしか probably
□ 〜ような気がする feel like
□ 公言する profess
□ 対象 object
□ 政教分離 separation of religion and state
□ 神を祀る enshrine a god
□ 現在に至る survive until today

The problem is that when asked if they believe in a particular religion, most Japanese answer in the negative, but when asked what religion their family has been traditionally associated with, they come up with the name of a sect.

Thus, while it is true that many Japanese profess no particular religious belief, it is also true that their ancestors have had some religious affiliation. In the Tokugawa period (1603-1868) the government required that all households be registered with a Buddhist temple, and in the Meiji period (1868-1912) Shinto was adopted as the state religion and all citizens considered its adherents. The statistics given above reflect this convoluted history, indicating not personal belief but ancestral association.

Q: Is Shinto the state religion of Japan?

While Shinto is the native religion of Japan, it was only in the Meiji period (1868-1912) that it became a state religion and the emperor designated a living god. After the defeat in World War II and the separation of religion and state, Shinto was relegated to the status of one of many religions. In the immediate postwar period, there were some 110,000 Shinto shrines throughout the country, most of which have survived until today as religious corporations.

Q: 靖国神社とは？

　靖国神社が他の神社と大きく異なるのは、祀られているのが国のために戦って亡くなった人という点です。

　この神社の**前身**は明治2(1869)年に明治天皇が建立した東京招魂社で、明治維新に到る戦いで亡くなった人々の霊を祀ることを目的としていました。明治12(1879)年に靖国神社と**改称**され、以来、**幕末**(1853年)から太平洋戦争までの100年近くの間に**戦没**した246.6万人を神霊として祀っています。このなかに、**いわゆる**東京裁判で敗戦後にA級戦犯として処刑された人々が、のちに含まれたことに対する**賛否両論**があります。また、政府要人の靖国参拝を中国と韓国がしばしば批判しています。

Q: 神社はお寺とどこが違うの？

　宗教上の違いは**種々**ありますが、最も大きな違いは神社ではお葬式を行わないという点です。その理由は、神道は遺体や遺骨を「ケ(穢れ)」として**忌み嫌う**ためです。したがって、神社にはお寺のように敷地内に墓地がありません。

　神道では「ケ」**に対する言葉**として「ハレ(晴れ)」を用います。「ハレ」は、神社の儀式やお祭りなどの非日常世界を意味しているのです。

- □ 前身　predecessor
- □ 改称する　rename
- □ 幕末　last days of Edo period
- □ 戦没する　be killed in a war
- □ いわゆる　as we say
- □ 賛否両論　arguments for and against
- □ 種々　many, a wide variety of
- □ 忌み嫌う　abhor
- □ 〜に対する言葉　antonym

Q: What is the significance of Yasukuni Shrine?

What distinguishes Yasukuni from other shrines is the fact that it is dedicated to those who died in the service of the Empire of Japan.

It was established in 1869 as Tokyo Shokonsha by Emperor Meiji to honor those who had died in fighting on behalf of the new Meiji government. It was renamed Yasukuni Shrine in 1879 and later rededicated to the spirits of the 2,466,000 people who had fallen in the service of the country from 1853 to the end of World War II. It came to include those executed as A-class war criminals by the Tokyo War Crimes Tribunal, giving rise to considerable controversy. The fact that government ministers occasionally visit the shrine to pay their respects to the spirits of Japanese soldiers, among others, is often an object of Chinese and South Korean criticism.

Q: What makes a Shinto shrine different from a Buddhist temple?

There are many theological as well as practical differences, but the most telling is that shrines do not conduct funerals. The reason is that Shinto avoids contact with the body and the remains of the deceased as being impure. This also explains why there are no graveyards within the compounds of Shinto shrines.

In contrast to the notion of impurity, there is the notion of the "bright." This refers to the world of the extraordinary as seen in Shinto rituals and festivals.

Q: 神社参拝は、どのように行うの？

神社の入り口に当るのが鳥居です。中央は神様の通り道とされるので、**なるべく**左右の端を通るようにするのが作法です。まず、御手洗で手を洗い、口の中も**すすぎ**ます。これは「**穢れ**」を落として神様の前に出ることを意味する重要な儀式です。

拝殿前に立ったら、軽くおじぎをして、**お賽銭**を入れ、鈴を鳴らし、2回おじぎをした後、2回**柏手を打ち**、最後にもう1回おじぎをして**退出**となります。これを「二礼二拍一礼」と言います。出雲大社のように四拍する神社もあり、あらかじめ参拝の作法を確認して出掛ける必要があります。

● 御手洗での作法
Purify your hands and mouth at the "*mitarashi/temizuya*" water pavilion

①柄杓を右手に持ち、左手に水をかけます。
First, take the ladle in your right hand, and pour water over your left hand.

②柄杓を左手に持ち替え、右手に水をかけます。
Switch hands and pour water over your right hand.

- □ 通り道 passage
- □ なるべく preferably
- □ すすぐ rinse
- □ 穢れ impurities
- □ お賽銭 donation
- □ 柏手を打つ clap one's hands in prayer
- □ 退出 withdraw

Q: What is the proper procedure for praying at a Shinto shrine?

The large gate (*torii*) in front of a shrine represents the entrance to the sacred compound. The center of the gate is reserved for the passage of the gods, so it is customary to make use of the left or right sides. Inside the compound, wash your hands and rinse your mouth with the water provided. This is an important ritual in that it removes impurities and indicates that one is ready to appear before the gods.

Standing before the shrine building, bow once lightly, leave a donation in the box provided, and ring the bell. Then bow twice, clap the hands twice, bow once more, and then withdraw. This is called the "two bows, two claps, one bow" system. Some shrines, such as Izumo Shrine, employ four claps or some other variation.

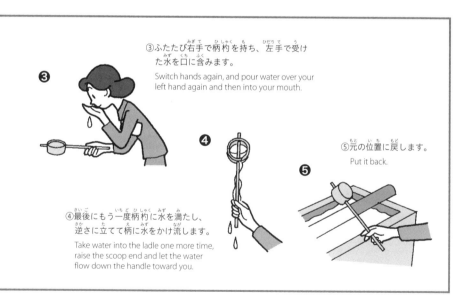

第2章 宗教

Q: 仏教には、どんな宗派があるの？

　仏教は、広くアジアで信仰されてきた宗教です。仏教発祥の地インドは今やヒンズー教徒が多数を占め、かつての仏教国・中国や韓国、北朝鮮は仏教と無縁の国になってしまっています。

　仏教徒が多くいるのは東南アジア諸国で、「小乗仏教」と呼ばれる宗派が主流です。この宗派は、僧侶になって自身の悟りを得ることを目的としています。一方、日本の仏教の主流になっているのが「大乗仏教」で、広く大衆を救う教えを基にしています。

　日本国内で活動している仏教の宗派は13とされていますが、信徒数が多いのは浄土宗、浄土真宗（本願寺派、大谷派）、真言宗、天台宗、日蓮宗、曹洞宗、臨済宗です。また、日蓮を宗祖とする創価学会は、形骸化した寺院から独立し、国内だけでなく海外192か国・地域に布教活動を展開している日本最大の信徒団体です。

Q: 禅とは、どんな教えなの？

　12、13世紀にかけて中国から渡来した宗派で、国内には臨済宗、曹洞宗などがあります。心から迷いを無くして、真理に到達するために瞑想をする、というのが基本的な教えで、そのために座禅という修行を行います。ただし、迷いを無くすというのは至難のわざで、欲望だらけの世界で生きる俗人には縁遠く、だからこそ座禅にあこがれる人がいるのかも知れません。

□ 発祥の地　birthplace
□ 無縁の　foreign
□ 悟りを得る　achieve enlightenment
□ 宗祖　founding father
□ 形骸化する　fall into moribund

□ 迷い　delusions
□ 真理に到達する　achieve enlightenment
□ 至難のわざ　insuperable difficulty
□ 俗人　layman
□ 縁遠く　far beyond

Q: How many Buddhist sects are there?

Buddhism is a religion that spread widely throughout Asia. Today, its country of origin, India, is largely populated by adherents of Hinduism, and in countries where Buddhism formerly thrived, such as China, South Korea, and North Korea, it is now a minor player.

Most Buddhist followers are in Southeast Asia and belong to the Hinayana school. In the Hinayana school the goal is to become a monk and achieve enlightenment. The Buddhism that came to Japan was the Mahayana, the goal of which is to save as many people as possible.

There are said to be 13 Buddhist sects in Japan, the ones with the most adherents being the Jodo, Jodo Shinshu (Hongan-ji and Otani branches), Shingon, Tendai, Nichiren, Soto, and Rinzai sects. The Soka Gakkai, which takes Nichiren as its founding father, broke off from its moribund parent body to spread widely not only in Japan but to 192 countries and territories throughout the world. It has since become Japan's largest religious organization.

Q: What is Zen Buddhism?

Coming to Japan in the 12th and 13th centuries from China, Zen now has two domestic sects, the Soto and the Rinzai. Zen's basic goal is to rid oneself of delusion and achieve enlightenment through meditation (*zazen*). The appeal of *zazen* lies in the almost insuperable difficulty of living without illusion in our modern materialistic world.

Q: 僧侶は、なぜ髪を剃っているの？

お寺の僧侶が髪を剃っているのは、**俗世を離れた**存在であることを示すためです。本来、仏教は悟りを得るための修行に出ることを「出家」といい、出家者は生涯**独身を貫か**ねばなりませんでした。その**覚悟を示す**ために髪を剃ったのです。ちなみに、カトリックの司祭などが頭のてっぺんの髪を丸く剃るのは、仏教の影響ともされます。

Q: お寺での参拝の作法は？

お寺の入り口が、山門です。この門を入る前に**合掌**して一礼します。本堂に向かう途中に手水場があるので、そこで手を洗い、口をすすぎ清めます。本堂前に**お線香をたく**香炉があれば、その煙を体に招いて**身を清め**ます。本堂では鐘がつるしてあればそれを鳴らし、お賽銭を入れ、**音を立てない**ように合掌し、頭を下げます。この時、願いごとを**念じ**ます。

❏ おみくじ

吉凶を書いた紙片のことで、神社や寺などで箱から直接引きます。吉凶を占う「おみくじ」は大吉以下、凶まで6種類が一般的です。吉札は持ち帰ってよいが、凶札は木の枝などに結び付けて帰ります。

- ❏ 俗世を離れる leave the mundane world
- ❏ 独身を貫く remain unmarried
- ❏ 覚悟を示す express one's determination
- ❏ 合掌する join one's hands in prayer
- ❏ お線香をたく burn incense
- ❏ 身を清める purify one's body
- ❏ 音を立てない soundless
- ❏ 念じる pray

Q: Why do Buddhist monks shave their heads?

Monks shave their heads as a sign that they have left the mundane world. Originally, monks had to leave their homes and families to embark on an unmarried journey of ascetic practice, and shaving their heads was a sign of their determination. It is said that the Catholic custom of priests' shaving the top of their heads is a Buddhist influence.

Q: What is the proper procedure for praying at a Buddhist temple?

The *sanmon* ("mountain gate") is the imposing entrance to a Buddhist temple, and before passing through it one places the hands together in prayer and bows lightly. Going toward the main hall, there will be a washbasin where the hands are washed and the mouth rinsed in an act of purification. Before the hall there may be a censer where incense is being burned; waft some of the incense toward your body to purify it. If there is a bell in front of the hall, ring it and place a donation in the box provided there. Then place one's hands soundlessly together in prayer and lower the head, while making a wish.

❏ What are *omikuji*?

Omikuji are fortunes written on small pieces of paper and drawn at random from a box at a temple or shrine. Commonly there are six types, from "great blessing" to "curse." Those indicating good fortune can be taken home, but less fortunate ones are tied to the branch of a nearby tree.

おみくじ
Omikuji

第3章 文化

山古志の棚田(新潟県) Tanada in Yamakoshi, Niigata

1 学芸

Q: 日本人のノーベル賞受賞者は？

物理学賞が10名、**化学賞**が7名、**医学生理学賞**が2名、**文学賞**が2名、**平和賞**が1名です(2014年現在)。

物理学賞：湯川秀樹(1949年)、朝永振一郎(1965年)、江崎玲於奈(1973年)、小柴昌俊(2002年)、小林誠・益川敏英・南部陽一郎(2008年)、赤崎勇・天野浩・中村修二(2014年)。

化学賞：福井謙一(1981年)、白川英樹(2000年)、野依良治(2001年)、田中耕一(2002年)、下村脩(2008年)、鈴木章・根岸英一(2010年)。

医学生理学賞：利根川進(1987年)、山中伸弥(2012年)。

文学賞：川端康成(1968年)、大江健三郎(1994年)。

平和賞：佐藤栄作(1974年)。

□ 受賞者 award winner
□ 物理学 physics
□ 化学 chemistry
□ 医学生理学 physiology of medicine
□ 文学 literature
□ 平和 peace

Chapter 3
Culture

1 Arts and Sciences

Q: How many Japanese have won the Nobel Prize?

There have been 10 winners in physics, 7 in chemistry, 2 in physiology of medicine, 2 in literature, and 1 for peace (as of 2014). The winners are as follows:

Physics: Hideki Yukawa (1949), Sin-Itiro Tomonaga (1965), Leona Esaki (1973), Masatoshi Koshiba (2002), Makoto Kobayashi, Toshihide Masukawa, and Yoichiro Nambu (2008), and Isamu Akasaki, Hiroshi Amano, and Shuji Nakamura (2014).
Chemistry: Kenichi Fukui (1981), Hideki Shirakawa (2000), Ryoji Noyori (2001), Koichi Tanaka (2002), Osamu Shimomura (2008), and Akira Suzuki and Ei-ichi Negishi (2010).
Physiology of medicine: Susumu Tonegawa (1987) and Shinya Yamanaka (2012).
Literature: Yasunari Kawabata (1968) and Kenzaburo Oe (1994).
Peace: Eisaku Sato (1974).

湯川秀樹
Hideki Yukawa

第3章 文化

Q: 文化勲章とは？

文化勲章とは、学術・芸術分野で貢献した人に与えられる、最も権威のある勲章です。学術分野では学士院会員など、芸術分野では芸術院会員などから選ばれるのが恒例ですが、ノーベル賞受賞者や外国人なども対象になります。1937年の創設以来、受章者は384名(2014年)で、うち外国人が5名(いずれも米国人)。

毎年、文化の日(11月3日)に皇居で授章式が行われています。

Q: 日本の代表的なマンガ家・アニメ作家は？

今やマンガとアニメーションは、日本文化の象徴の一つです。日本のマンガ家やアニメ作家に大きな影響を与えた人物としては、手塚治虫(1928–89)が挙げられます。代表作の一つの『鉄腕アトム』はアニメ化されて、米国では『アストロボーイ』というタイトルでテレビ放映され、人気を博しました。その後、日本のアニメ作品が世界各地で評判になり、"anime"という言葉が英語として定着するまでになりました。

アニメ作家として傑出しているのは宮崎駿(1941–)で、2001年に発表した『千と千尋の神隠し』は観客動員2350万人、興行収入304億円という日本映画史上での最高記録を樹立しました。

この作品はベルリン国際音楽祭で金熊賞(2002年)、アカデミー賞長編アニメ賞(2003年)を受賞し、日本人で二人目のアカデミー名誉賞(2014年)に輝きました。

□ 貢献する　contribute
□ 権威のある　prestigious
□ 恒例　customary
□ 影響を与える　impact on
□ 人気を博す　become popular
□ 傑出する　outstand
□ 樹立する　establish
□ 輝く　win (an award)

Q: What is the Order of Culture?

The Order of Culture is the most prestigious Japanese award for contributions to Japanese art, literature, and culture. In the sciences it is customary for candidates to be chosen from among members of the Japan Academy, and in the arts from the Academy of Arts, but non-Japanese and Nobel Prize winners are also considered. The Order was established in 1937, and to date (2014) 384 people have received the award, among whom there have been 5 foreigners (all citizens of the United States).

The awards ceremony is held every year in the imperial palace on Culture Day (November 3).

Q: Who are the most famous Japanese manga and anime artists?

Without a doubt, manga and anime have now become two of the most representative arts of Japan. The person who had the greatest impact on these arts is Osamu Tezuka (1928-89). His celebrated manga *Tetsuwan Atomu* was made into an anime and telecast in the United States under the title *Astro Boy* to great acclaim. Subsequently, Japanese animation won kudos throughout the world to such an extent that "anime" became a part of the English language.

Today the most outstanding anime artist is Hayao Miyazaki (b. 1941). His *Spirited Away* (2001) attracted 23,500,000 theatergoers and grossed ¥30.4 billion, making it the most successful film in Japanese history.

It won the Golden Bear at the 2002 Berlin International Film Festival and the 2003 Academy Award for Best Animated Feature, with Miyazaki becoming the second Japanese to win an Honorary Academy Award in 2014.

Q: 世界的に有名な映画監督は？

日本人初のアカデミー名誉賞(1990年)を受賞した黒澤明(1910-98)は、スティーヴン・スピルバーグ、ジョージ・ルーカス、フランシス・フォード・コッポラなどの海外の映画人にも大きな影響を与え"世界のクロサワ"と呼ばれました。黒澤作品はダイナミックな映像表現とヒューマニズムあふれる作風で『羅生門』(1950年)以降、『生きる』(52年)、『七人の侍』(54年)など約30作が発表されました。

映画手法で世界的に影響を与えたのが小津安二郎(1903-63)で、代表作は『晩春』(49年)、『東京物語』(53年)です。

日本映画は1960年代からテレビに押されて低調になり、人気はアニメ作品に移ってきていますが、近年は新しい映像作家も出現しています。海外で高い評価をされているのは北野武(1947–)で、コメディアンとして活躍する一方、1989年に映画監督としてデビュー後、『HANA-BI』でベネチア国際映画祭でグランプリ(97年)を獲得するなど、**日本を代表する**映画人の一人とされます。

- 映画人 cineast
- あふれる rich
- 〜に押されて lose ground to
- 低調 slumping
- 日本を代表する Japan's most renowned

Q: Who is the most famous Japanese film director?

Akira Kurosawa (1910-98) was the first Japanese to win an Honorary Academy Award (1990) and is known for the influence he exercised on Steven Spielberg, George Lucas, and Francis Ford Coppola. It was said at the time that Kurosawa was not just a Japanese director but a director for the whole world. His works are characterized by their dynamism and humanitarianism, starting with *Rashomon* (1950), *Ikiru* (1952), and *Seven Samurai* (1954). In all, he directed some 30 movies.

The director who exercised great global influence in terms of technique was Yasujiro Ozu (1903-63). His most memorable works are *Late Spring* (1949) and *Tokyo Story* (1953).

In the 1960s the film industry began to lose ground to television, with anime gaining in popularity, but just recently new film creators have come to the fore. Abroad, Takeshi Kitano (b. 1947) is highly rated. While continuing his career as a comedian, he debuted as a movie director in 1989 and won the Golden Lion at the Venice Film Festival for *Hana-bi* (Fireworks) in 1997, among others. He is now one of Japan's most renowned directors.

Q: 世界で評価が高い音楽家は？

戦後、多くの若い音楽家が海外のコンクールに挑戦してきましたが、その**先駆者**として挙げられるのが指揮者の小沢征爾(1935-)です。73年から30**年間にわたって**ボストン交響楽団(米国)の音楽監督を務めたほか、2002年にはウィーン国立歌劇場(イタリア)の音楽監督に就任し、世界の**音楽界**で**話題になり**ました。

クラシック界では、米国を**拠点**に活動しているバイオリンの五嶋みどり(1971-)、英国在住のピアノの内田光子(1948-)、イタリアで高い評価を得ているソプラノの中丸三千繪(1960-)などがいます。また、日本人初のアカデミー賞作曲賞を受賞(1987年)した坂本龍一(1952-)、シンセサイザーによる作曲や演奏を行っている冨田勲(1932-2016)などが**世界的に知られ**ています。

- □ 先駆者　forerunner
- □ ～年間にわたって　for ~ years
- □ 音楽界　music world
- □ 話題になる　get into the news
- □ 拠点　base
- □ 世界的に知られる　be known globally

Q: Who are Japan's most acclaimed world musicians?

Since the end of the war, while many Japanese young people have gone abroad to enter music competitions, the forerunner of them all is surely the conductor Seiji Ozawa (b. 1935). He became the music director of the Boston Symphony Orchestra in 1973 and served in that position for nearly 30 years. From 2002 to 2010 he was the principal conductor of the Vienna State Opera.

In classical music, there is the US-based violinist Midori Goto (b. 1971), the naturalized-British pianist Mitsuko Uchida (b. 1948), and the Italy-acclaimed soprano Michie Nakamaru (b. 1960). Ryuichi Sakamoto (b. 1952) won an Academy Award for the Best Original Score in 1987, and Isao Tomita (1932–2016) is known globally for his composing and playing on the synthesizer.

ウィーン国立歌劇場　Vienna State Opera

Q: 日本画は西洋の絵とどう違うの？

　日本画という言葉は、明治以降に西洋の絵を洋画といったことに対してつくられたものです。最大の違いは材料で、鉱物をくだいて粉末状にした**岩絵の具**を、**にかわ**を**媒材**にして紙や絹に描きます。使う材料によって色彩の**ぼかし**方などの表現方法が異なるため、油絵など西洋の絵と比べて技法を習得するまでに**修練**が必要です。

　日本画は花鳥風月といわれるように、自然を主題にしたものが多く見られます。しかし、こうした伝統を受け継ぎながらも、新しい日本画をつくろうという**試み**もされてきました。

　国内外で高く評価されている現代の日本画家の一人が平山郁夫（1930–2009）で、仏教に関わる作品を数多く発表しました。フランス、中国、フィリピン、韓国などの**国家顕彰**も受けています。

- 岩絵の具　natural mineral pigments
- にかわ　glue
- 媒材　medium, binder
- ぼかす　gradate
- 修練　training and practice
- 試み　endeavor
- 国家顕彰　award from the national government

Q: What is the difference between Japanese painting and Western painting?

The term "Japanese painting" (*Nihonga*) was coined in the Meiji period (1868-1912) to distinguish Japanese-style painting from Western-style painting (*Yoga*). The most telling difference is in the materials used. Japanese painting makes use of minerals and other natural materials that have been powdered into fine pigments, which are applied to Japanese paper (*washi*) or silk with a glue binder made of hide. Depending on the materials used, the way in which shading and gradation is created differs, meaning that, compared to Western oil painting, considerable training and practice are required for mastery.

Japanese painting most often takes nature as its theme, as indicated by the phrase *kachofugetsu* (flowers, birds, wind, and moon), a common literary reference to nature. While this traditional approach is still being followed, there are also endeavors to create something new.

Within Japan Ikuo Hirayama (1930-2009) garnered recognition for his many depictions of Buddhist themes. He also won awards in France, China, the Philippines, South Korea, and elsewhere.

平山郁夫の日本画
Japanese painting (*nihonga*) by Ikuo Hirayama

2 伝統技芸

Q: 歌舞伎はいつから始まったの？

17世紀初め、出雲大社の巫女と称する阿国が京都で演じた「かぶき踊り」が起源とされます。しかし、これが奇抜で煽情的だったため、風俗を乱すとして幕府が禁じました。後年、女性役を演じる男優（女形）を配することで存続を図ろうという動きが出て、元禄期（1688～1704年）に現在のスタイルが確立しました。

歌舞伎役者は原則的に世襲制で、3歳頃から子役としてデビューし、役柄や名前も伝統的に引き継ぐ慣わしです。例えば、歌舞伎界で権威が高い市川家の場合は、新之助～海老蔵～団十郎という形で襲名し、荒々しく豪快な役柄を演じる「荒事」を得意とします。

❏ **隈取**

歌舞伎は様式性が高い演劇で、それを端的に表現しているのが役の化粧。主役が顔に描く「隈取」は、役柄を観客が理解しやすいようにした舞台芸術の一つです。

- ❏ ～と称する proclaim oneself
- ❏ 風俗を乱す disrupt a social norm
- ❏ 配する cast
- ❏ 存続を図る make an effort to preserve
- ❏ ～という動きが出る start on
- ❏ 世襲制 hereditary succession
- ❏ 権威が高い authoritative
- ❏ 襲名する succeed to someone's stage name
- ❏ 端的に clearly

2 Traditional Theater and Handicrafts

Q: What are the roots of the Kabuki theater?

Kabuki is said to have been first performed in Kyoto by a maiden (or shaman) named Okuni from the Izumo Shrine at the beginning of the 17th century. However, since Kabuki was viewed not only as bizarre but as erotic and disruptive of social norms, the government soon banned it. Subsequently, efforts were made to preserve Kabuki by having men play the female roles, and in the Genroku era (1688-1704) Kabuki as we know it today came into being.

As a rule, Kabuki is based on hereditary succession, with a child first appearing on the stage at the age of three and inheriting the type of role played and eventually the name of his father. For example, in the famous Ichikawa family, the names Shinosuke, Ebizo, and Danjuro have been passed on from generation to generation, along with its dynamic, exaggerated style of acting known as *aragoto*.

❑ *Kumadori* Makeup

Kabuki is highly stylized, and this is clearly seen in the actor's makeup (*kumadori*). Through this distinctive makeup, the audience is able to easily identify the character of the actor.

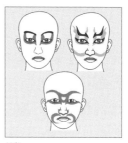

隈取 *Kumadori* Makeup

Q: 歌舞伎はどこでやっているの？

歌舞伎公演のメッカは、東京の歌舞伎座です。2013年に改築オープンした新劇場は、座席数約1800のバリアフリー設備が整った施設です。**興行**は月ごとに**演目**が変わり、原則として昼の部、夜の部の一日２公演が行われます。

また、新橋演舞場（東京）、大阪松竹座、京都四條南座などでも定期的に公演されています。

Q: 能と狂言はどんな関係なの？

いずれも奈良時代頃に中国から渡来した、**滑稽な**仕草をするサーカスのような芸能である「散楽」がルーツで、そのうちの歌舞が能、物まねが狂言に発展したとされます。

能は鎌倉時代に現在の原型が整い、14世紀後半に観阿弥・世阿弥父子によって芸術性の高い演劇へと**昇華**しました。**主役**(シテ)がつける面は、**演者**の表情を隠すことで非日常性と様式美を高める**効果をねらって**います。

能が非日常的な悲劇をテーマにしているのに対し、狂言は風刺や滑稽を強調した**写実的**な喜劇です。能と狂言は**表裏一体**の関係で、能舞台では**たいてい**能、狂言、能という順序で上演されます。

□ 興行 performance
□ 演目 program
□ 滑稽な humorous
□ 昇華する make the next leap
□ 主役 protagonist
□ 演者 actor
□ 効果を狙う aim an effect
□ 写実的な realistic
□ 表裏一体 two sides of the same coin
□ たいてい generally

Q: Where is Kabuki performed?

The Mecca of Kabuki performance is the Kabuki-za in Tokyo. The new theater, rebuilt and opened to the public in 2013, is a barrier-free structure that accommodates 1,800 people. The program changes every month, with different plays comprising the afternoon and evening performances.

歌舞伎座(東京都)
Kabukiza theatre, Tokyo

Performances are also held regularly at Tokyo's Shimbashi Enbujo, the Osaka Shochiku-za, and the Kyoto Shijo Minami-za.

Q: What is the relationship between Noh and Kyogen?

Both Noh and Kyogen are forms of classical drama originating in circus-like antics called *sangaku* that made their way to Japan from China in the Nara period (710-784). It is speculated that the singing and dancing aspects of *sangaku* developed into Noh, and the pantomime aspects became Kyogen.

Noh assumed its present-day form in the Kamakura period (1185-1333) and in late 14th century under the father and son Kan'ami and Zeami, who raised it to a highly artistic form of theater. The mask worn by the protagonist (*shite*) has the effect of concealing the actor's individual features and lending an otherworldly mystique to the performance.

In contrast to Noh's otherworldliness, Kyogen is realistic and deals in satire and comedy. Kyogen and Noh are, so to speak, two sides of the same coin, and the order in which they are performed is Noh, Kyogen, Noh.

能(左)
狂言(右)
Noh (l.), Kyogen (r.)

第3章 文化

Q: 文楽とはどんな芸能なの？

　日本特有の人形芝居です。浄瑠璃という音楽と語りに合わせ、1体の人形を3人で操ります。文楽は江戸時代に全国的に流行し、17世紀終わり頃に竹本義太夫によってさらに高度な芸能として**確立**しました。2002年にはユネスコの世界無形文化遺産に登録されました。現在、東京では国立劇場、大阪では国立文楽劇場で定期的に公演が行われています。

Q: 落語と講談の違いは？

　話芸を職業とする人が登場したのは江戸時代で、それは**戦乱**のない平和な世の中になったことの反映でした。落語は噺家と呼ばれる人が滑稽な話をして客を笑わせ、講談は講釈師が**戦記**や**人情話**で客を泣かせるといった違いがあります。

　また、落語と講談はそれぞれ江戸（東京）と上方（大阪）でも違いがあります。その一例が、演者が使う道具です。江戸落語の噺家は扇子と手ぬぐいを**小道具**に使いますが、上方落語では小拍子（拍子木）も小道具として使うほか噺家の前に見台（机）・膝隠し（衝立）を置きます。講談でも、東京の講釈師は張り扇を小道具にしますが、大阪では張り扇と拍子木を**併用**します。

□ 操る　manipurate
□ 確立する　achieve wide popularity
□ 戦乱　war
□ 戦記　war story
□ 人情話　sentimental tale
□ 小道具　stage prop
□ 〜を併用する　use 〜 together

Q: What is Bunraku?

Bunraku is a type of puppet theater unique to Japan. Accompanied by music and narration called *Joruri*, each puppet on the stage is worked by three puppeteers. Bunraku achieved wide popularity in the Edo period (1603-1868), and near the end of the 18th century Takemoto Gidayu elevated it to the highly refined art it is today. In 2002 UNESCO recognized Bunraku as an Intangible Cultural Heritage of Humanity. Performances are periodically held at the National Theater in Tokyo and the National Bunraku Theatre in Osaka.

文楽人形
Bunraku puppet

Q: What is the difference between Rakugo and Kodan?

Verbal or oral arts first made their appearance in the Edo period (1603-1868). They were a product of newly arrived peace, after more than a century of civil war. In Rakugo, the performer tells a humorous story that makes the audience laugh; in Kodan, the performer narrates war stories and sentimental tales that make the audience cry. This is the principal difference in terms of content.

There are also differences between Osaka and Tokyo. One example of this is the difference in props. In Tokyo the Rakugo performer uses a folding fan and a small towel, whereas in Osaka the performer adds to this a pair of wooden clappers as well as a lectern in front of him and partition before the knees. In Tokyo the Kodan performer uses a pleated paper fan to establish rhythm, but in Osaka both clappers and pleated fans are used.

第3章 文化

Q: 生け花って、なに？

　植物を主に、さまざまな材料と組み合わせて構成して鑑賞をする、日本発祥の芸術です。室町時代中期頃から僧侶が仏前に供える献花として考案したものが、後に華道として**伝承される**ようになり、江戸時代後期に多くの流派が生まれました。現代では、伝統様式や技法にこだわらない生け花も登場しています。

Q: 日本人は誰でも茶道の心得があるの？

　生け花（華道）と共に江戸時代から戦前までの日本女性**必須**の**たしなみ**とされてきた茶道は、現代では一部の人が行っていて一般的ではありません。したがって、茶道のしきたりなどを**心得ている**日本人は**ごく少数**です。

　現代に継承されている茶道の原点は、16世紀後期に簡素な美を**追求**することをめざした千利休の侘び茶です。

　茶道は客をもてなす作法で、主人は**茶室**で沸かした湯で抹茶（茶葉を粉末にしたもの）を**かき混ぜ**客に飲んでもらいます。そのプロセスを点前と言い、この**所作**が茶道の**極意**とされます。茶室は、主人と客との心の交流の場なのです。

□ 伝承される　be transmitted
□ 必須の　required
□ たしなみ　accomplishment
□ 心得ている　aquainted
□ ごく少数　small minority
□ 追求する　pursue
□ 茶室　tea-ceremony house
□ かき混ぜる　mix
□ 所作　process
□ 極意　essence

Q: What is ikebana?

Ikebana is the uniquely Japanese art of arranging flowers and sometimes other material in a form worthy of aesthetic appreciation. It began in the mid Muromachi period (1336-92) with monks arranging flowers before Buddhist statues, to be transmitted to later generations as *kado* (the way of flowers), producing a proliferation of different schools in the late Edo period (1603-1868). Now, in addition to the traditional forms of arrangement, entirely new styles have come into being.

生け花
Ikebana

Q: Is every Japanese familiar with the principles of the Way of Tea?

From the Edo period until the Pacific War, the Way of Tea—that is, the Japanese tea ceremony—was one of those cultural refinements that all Japanese women were expected to possess, along with the art of flower arranging. Now, however, it is carried out by only a small minority, its principles no longer widely known.

茶道
Way of tea

The tea ceremony practiced today has its roots in the work of Sen no Rikyu (1522-91), who stressed rustic simplicity and directness of approach (*wabicha*).

The tea ceremony consists of the interplay between host and guests: the host boils the water, mixes in powdered green tea leaves, and has the guests drink the resultant tea. This process is called *temae* and represents the essence of the Way of Tea. The tearoom is the venue for this harmonious meeting of minds between host and guest.

第3章 文化

Q: 家元制度って、なに？

茶道や華道などの日本の伝統技芸には、それを**代々継承**してきた家元が存在します。例えば茶道では、千利休**を祖とする**表千家、裏千家、武者小路千家の3家があります。

伝統技芸は**相伝**といって師匠が弟子に一対一で極意を伝えるのを原則とします。家元制度は相伝において**血縁**を重視しています。

Q: 陶磁器と漆器の違いは？

日本の伝統工芸品といえば陶磁器と漆器です。その違いは、器の素材にあります。陶磁器は土、漆器は木がベースで漆でコーティングされています。また、陶磁器は粘土を焼き、漆器は木に漆を**塗り重ねる**ため、それぞれ「焼き物」「塗り物」と呼ばれます。

陶磁器は、有色粘土で形を作り**釉薬**を塗って1100〜1300℃で焼いた陶器と、白色粘土で形を作り1300〜1400℃で焼いた磁器があり、これらは中国伝来の技術をもとに発展しました。かつて欧米では陶磁器を"China"、漆器を"Japan"と呼びました。

□ 代々 from one generation to another
□ 継承する inherit
□ 〜を祖とする be founded by
□ 相伝 hereditary succession
□ 血縁 bloodline
□ 塗り重ねる coat multiply
□ 釉薬 glaze

Q: What is the *iemoto* system?

In ikebana, the Way of Tea, and other traditional arts, there is a "house" (*iemoto*), or more broadly a grand master, who carries on the tradition from one generation to another. For example, in the tea ceremony there are three houses: the Omote Senke, Ura Senke, and Mushanokoji Senke, all of which trace their history back to Sen no Rikyu.

In this system the essence of the tradition is passed down from master to disciple in a strictly hereditary fashion, placing ultimate emphasis on bloodline.

Q: What is the difference between ceramic ware and lacquer ware?

Among Japanese handicrafts, ceramic and lacquer wares are two of the stars. The difference between them lies in the materials used. Ceramics are made of clay, while lacquer ware is built on a wooden base on which coatings of lacquer are applied. Further, since ceramics is made of fired clay, it is called "fired ware" (*yakimono*), while lacquer ware is made of multiple coatings of lacquer and is therefore called "coated ware" (*nurimono*).

Ceramics created from colored clay, glazed, and fired at temperatures between 1100 and 1300 degrees is earthenware (*toki*), and that made of white clay and fired between 1300 and 1400 degrees is porcelain (*jiki*). Both of these were introduced from China and further developed in Japan. In the past, porcelain was often referred to as "China" in Western countries, and lacquer ware as "Japan."

漆器
Lacquer ware

陶磁器
Ceramic ware

Q: 日本刀の特徴は？

日本に鉄器の製法が伝来したのは古墳時代以前で、砂鉄を原料にした「たたら製鉄」という技法がもとになって、武器としての刀がつくられるようになりました。現在、日本刀と呼ばれるものは平安時代末期以降の刀剣で、長さによって太刀（刀）、脇差、短刀に大別されます。

日本刀には殺傷力を高めるために鉄を鍛錬して堅固なものにする技術と共に、形やデザインの美しさも求められました。実用性と芸術性を併せ持つことが、日本刀の特徴なのです。

戦乱がおさまった江戸時代、刀は実用性よりも芸術性を追求するようになったため、慶長年間（1596〜1614年）以前のものを古刀、それ以後から明治8年までのものを新刀、明治9年（廃刀令が出た年）以降につくられたものを現代刀と称しています。

日本刀 Japanese sword

❏ 刀工

日本刀は現代でも美術工芸品としてつくられていて、なかには人間国宝に認定される刀工もいます。

- □ 伝来する　imported
- □ 殺傷力　killing power
- □ 鍛錬する　temper
- □ 堅固な　strong
- □ 併せ持つ　combine
- □ 戦乱がおさまる　a war is at an end
- □ 人間国宝　living national treasure

Q: What are the outstanding characteristics of a Japanese sword?

The techniques for manufacturing ironware first came to Japan sometime before the Kofun period (around 250-538) and made use of iron sand in a furnace called a *tatara*. From this emerged the first swords. What is now called the Japanese sword (*Nihon-to*) appeared on the stage of history in the late Heian period (794-1185), and can be classified according to length (from long to short) as *tachi*, *wakizashi*, and *tanto*.

The Japanese sword not only requires proper tempering to make it a lethal weapon but is also expected to have an aesthetically pleasing form and design. This combination of practicality and beauty is what distinguishes the Japanese sword.

With the coming of peace in the Edo period, the aesthetic element came to be more valued than the practical. As a result, swords made before the Keicho era (1596-1614) are now called *Koto* (Old Swords); those made thereafter until 1875 are called *Shinto* (New Swords). Swords made after the wearing of swords in public was banned in 1876 are called *Gendai-to* (Modern Swords).

❏ Swordsmiths

Swords are still being made in modern Japan as one of its highly valued arts and crafts. In fact, some swordsmiths have been designated living national treasures by the government.

江戸時代の刀工
Japanese swordsmith in the Edo period

Q: 人間国宝って、なに？

文部科学大臣が指定する重要無形文化財保持者(個人、団体)の通称で、芸能部門では延べ177名、工芸技術部門では延べ173名が認定されています(2014年)。ちなみに、これまでに刀工は6名、落語家は3名が人間国宝に認定されました。

Q: 大相撲はいつから始まったの？

力比べという形で神意(神様の意思)をうかがう儀式として古代から行われ、史実に記録されている最初は642年とされます。平安時代には天皇の前で相撲大会(節会)が開催されました。

江戸時代になると、神社の祭礼の際の興行として催されるようになりました。大名が力自慢の人を家来にして競わせ、力士番付が流行しました。明治時代の「裸体禁止令」で存続の危機を迎えましたが、相撲好きの明治天皇によって国技とされ現在に至っています。

Q: 大相撲はいつ、どこでやっているの？

本場所(15日間興行)は、年6回開催されています。国技館(東京)では1月・5月・9月の3場所が、他は大阪場所(3月)、名古屋場所(7月)、九州場所(11月)です。本場所以外は、地方巡業やチャリティ興行などが行われています。

- □ 延べ the total number of
- □ 神意をうかがう ask about divine will
- □ 史実 historical document
- □ 番付 ranking
- □ 存続の危機 crisis of existence
- □ 国技 national sport
- □ 地方巡業 exhibitions in the provinces

Q: What is a Living National Treasure?

A Living National Treasure refers to an individual or group considered as possessing an important intangible cultural property as designated by the Minister of Education. In the performing arts there are 177 holders of this title, and in arts and crafts 173 (as of 2014). Six swordsmiths and three Rakugo performers are among this number.

Q: When was the first sumo bout?

As a type of wrestling, sumo was practiced in ancient times as a means of divining the will of the gods. It is first mentioned in historical documents in 642. It is said that in the Heian period (794-1185), sumo tournaments (called *sechie*) were held before the emperor.

In the Edo period (1603-1868) sumo became one of the events conducted at Shinto festivals. Feudal lords of the time would compete by having the strongest of their vassals battle it out in the ring, and published rankings of the strongest wrestlers became popular. In the Meiji period (1868-1912) sumo faced a crisis when public nakedness was banned, but that was overcome when Emperor Meiji named sumo the national sport.

Q: When and where are sumo tournaments held?

Fifteen-day tournaments are held six times a year. Three tournaments are held at the Kokugikan in Tokyo (January, May, and September), one in Osaka (March), one in Nagoya (July), and one in Fukuoka, Kyushu (November). Bouts also take place as exhibitions in the provinces and as charity events.

両国国技館(東京都)
Ryogoku kokugikan, Tokyo

第3章 文化

Q: 力士になるには？

　新弟子検査に合格しなければなりません。原則として身長173cm以上、体重75kg以上の体格が必要で、外国人も対象になります。新弟子は国技館内の相撲教習所で6カ月間教習を受けますが、試験はありません。序ノ口から幕下までの4階級は養成員とされ、所属部屋に養成費(月額20万円程度)が相撲協会から支給されます。十両から横綱までの6階級(定員70名)の関取には月給(100〜282万円)と賞与や場所ごとの報奨金などが支給されます。

土俵入り Dohyo-iri

Q: 柔道と空手の違いは？

　柔道は、柔術という古武道をもとに1882年に加納治五郎によって創始され、投げ技、固め技があります。試合時間は3〜20分間で、延長もあります。一本、技あり、有効、効果の順でスコアがつき、勝負が決まります。1964年の東京五輪で正式種目に採用されて以来、国際競技になりました。柔道着は元は白一色でしたが、近年は青色の柔道着も普及しています。

□ 新弟子 new apprentice　　　□ 創始する create
□ 教習 instruction　　　　　　□ 勝負が決まる decide a game
□ 部屋 sumo stable

Q: What are the requirements for becoming a sumo wrestler?

First of all, new hopefuls must pass a physical exam, proving they are at least 173 centimeters tall and not less than 75 kilograms in weight. The same applies to foreign applicants. New recruits must then attend a sumo school within the Kokugikan in Tokyo for six months, although there are no tests. Wrestlers in the first four of the six divisions in sumo are considered trainees, and the Sumo Association pays the stables to which they belong a monthly fee of some ¥200,000. The 70 wrestlers in the six ranks from *juryo* to *yokozuna* receive a monthly salary of from ¥1,000,000 to ¥2,820,000 plus a bonus for each tournament they participate in.

Q: What is the difference between judo and karate?

Judo was created by Jigoro Kano in 1882 on the basis of an old martial art known as jujutsu. It consists of throwing and grappling techniques. The time of the match is from three to twenty minutes, with extensions possible. Scoring is based on, in descending order, *ippon*, *waza-ari*, *yuko*, and *koka*. Since being

柔道 Judo

chosen as one of the events in the 1964 Tokyo Olympics, judo has become an international sport. The judo uniform (*judogi*) was formerly exclusively white in color, but recently blue has also come into use.

空手は、沖縄で発達した**護身用**の武技で、中国拳法の影響を受けたことから"唐手"とも呼ばれました。突き、打ち、当て、蹴りを技の基本とし、競技は3分間で3**本先取**による「組手試合」、攻防の技の**組合せ**を競う「型試合」の2種があります。空手着は、柔道着を改良したものです。

空手 Karate

Q: 剣道の勝負はどうつけるの？

剣道は、江戸時代に武士が鍛錬のために行っていた剣術が競技として発展したものです。竹刀で相手の防具の面・胴・小手を打つか、喉を突くかすれば「一本」となります。試合では5分間で二本先取りの勝負が3回行われ、勝敗を決めます。

剣道で強調される「礼に始まって礼に終わる」は、他の伝統技芸でも共通の基本精神です。

- □ 護身用の as a means of self-defense
- □ 〜本先取 get 〜 points first
- □ 組合せ combination
- □ 〜着 uniform of
- □ 礼 respect

Karate ("empty hand") is a martial art that developed in Okinawa as a means of self-defense. From the fact that it was influenced by Chinese *kenpo*, the name is sometimes written with the Chinese characters that mean "Tang (dynasty) hand." Its principal techniques are punching, striking, and kicking. A bout runs for three minutes, with the winner decided by the first to get three points. There are two modes in karate: *kumite* (contact sparring) and *kata* (a formalized sequence of movements representing various offensive and defensive postures). The uniform (*karategi*) is a modification of the judo uniform.

Q: How is the winner decided in kendo?

Kendo (Way of the Sword) is a martial art that developed in the Edo period (1603-1868) as a way for samurai to practice sword fighting (*kenjutsu*). It uses bamboo swords (*shinai*) and protective armor, and a point is scored when the opponent is struck on the headpiece, breastplate, or *kote* (covering for forearms, wrists, and hands) or when a successful thrust is made to the throat. One bout consists of five minutes (there are three bouts in all), and the winner is the first to win two points.

As in the other traditional martial arts, kendo emphasizes respect for one's opponent: "A match commences with a show of respect and concludes with a show of respect."

剣道 Kendo

Q: アーチェリーと弓道の違いは？

弓で矢を射て的に当てる、という点では同じですが、弓の構造が違います。アーチェリーの弓は、弓道の和弓とは異なって**精度を向上**させる機械的な構造を持っていて、日本では洋弓とも呼ばれます。

また、競技のうえではアーチェリーが的中率のみを重視するのに対して、弓道では**射手**のフォームも得点の対象になります。弓道の試合は、主に屋内で行う「近的」（射距離28ｍ、的径36cm）、主に屋外で行う「遠的」（射距離60ｍ、的径1ｍ）の2種に大別されます。

Q: 囲碁、将棋のプロ棋士とは？

日本では、趣味として囲碁や将棋を楽しむ人が大勢います。一方、職業として行っているのが「棋士」です。では、プロ棋士になるにはどうすればよいでしょうか。

囲碁の場合は、まず入段試験に合格しなければなりません。受験者のほとんどは子どもの頃から師匠のもとで修業をしてきた人で、合格率は**例年**約60名の受験者の1割程度です。試験に合格して初段になった後は、棋戦での**勝星**数・タイトル戦でのタイトル獲得数・賞金ランキングによって**昇段**し、九段まで昇段できるのは一部の人です。

□ 矢を射る shoot a bow
□ 精度を向上させる improve accuracy
□ 射手 shooter
□ 例年 typical year
□ 〜程度 about
□ 勝星 victory
□ 昇段する advance to higher rank

Q: What is the difference between Japanese archery (*kyudo*) and Western archery?

The aim of both is to hit a target, but the structure of the bow is different. In contrast to the unadorned Japanese bow (*wakyu*), Western bows (*yokyu*) are often equipped with mechanical aids to improve accuracy.

In competition, Western archery is scored on accuracy alone, but Japanese archery also takes form into account. Matches can be classified into whether they take place indoors (distance 28 meters, target diameter 36 centimeters) or outdoors (distance 60 meters, target diameter 1 meter).

弓道 Japanese archery (*kyudo*)

Q: What does it take to become a professional go or shogi player?

Go and shogi are two popular board games with many hobbyist followers, but there are also professional players called *kishi*. How does one become a professional?

In go, the first step is to pass an entrance exam. Even though most examinees have been training under a professional since childhood, only about 10% pass the test on a typical year, with some 60 taking the exam. Successful applicants are then ranked as a first *dan* (rank), and further advancement depends on games won, victories in title matches, and prize money ranking. The highest rank is 9th *dan*, which very few people reach.

囲碁 Go

第3章 文化

　将棋の場合は、まず日本将棋連盟の養成機関である「奨励会」に入ることが条件です。会員同士の対局成績によって、満21歳までに初段、満26歳までに四段にならないと退会となり、プロ棋士への道は閉ざされます。プロ棋士は四段から九段までの段位の人で、毎年、戦績に応じて5段階に分かれたリーグ戦で順位が付けられます。最上位のA級のリーグ戦の優勝者には名人への挑戦権が与えられます。

Q: 競技かるたは、どんなゲームなの？

　100枚ずつ対になった200枚の札を使う集中力を必要とするゲームです。読み札（絵札）には、13世紀の和歌集から選ばれた和歌と絵が、対の取り札（文字札）には下の句が記されます。読み札が読まれると、対戦する2人が取り札を取り合う競技で、優れた記憶力と反射神経が求められます。女性は和服に袴を着けて対戦しますが、そのしとやかさは競技の場ではバトルモードに一転します。

　段位は初段から十段まであり、四段以上（A級）が全国大会への出場資格があります。競技かるた人口は小学生からお年寄りまで幅広く、毎年1月に開催される名人位・クイーン位決定戦では、頂点となる男女2名が決まります。

□ 退会　withdrawal
□ 〜への道が閉ざされる　road to becoming 〜 is closed
□ しとやかさ　graceful
□ 一転する　change quickly
□ 幅広い　wide range of
□ 頂点　champion

In shogi, the first requirement is to gain entrance to the Shoreikai, an organization that trains professional shogi players and is run by the Japan Shogi Association. Members play against one another until they reach the 1st *dan* level by the age of 21 and 4th *dan* level by the age of 26. Barring this, they must leave the Shoreikai and the road to becoming a professional player is closed. Professional players are ranked from 4th to 9th *dan*. Winners of A-league tournaments gain the right to challenge the current holder of the title of Meijin, the most prestigious title in Japanese professional shogi.

将棋 Shogi

Q: What is competitive *karuta*?

Karuta is a card game of concentration. There are 200 cards in groups of 100 cards each. One card (the reading card) has the text from a poem taken from a 13th-century poetry anthology (*Hyakunin Isshu*) and an illustration. The other card (the grabbing card) has the last part of the poem. When the text is read from the reading card, two competing players strive to see who can touch the appropriate grabbing card first. The game is a test of the powers of concentration as well of quick response. Women wear graceful kimonos, but quickly go into battle mode.

In tournament or competitive *karuta*, rankings are from 1st *dan* to 10th, and players with a 4th *dan* or higher can take part in national tournaments. The large competitive *karuta* population ranges from elementary school children to the elderly, and every year in January a tournament is held to see who will be honored with the title of Meijin (for men) or Queen (for women).

小倉百人一首
Ogura hyakunin isshu

3 現代の文化の特徴

Q: 今の日本文化の特徴は？

　昔からの伝統文化と欧米風の生活習慣が**混在**するのが、現代の日本文化の特徴です。日本人は昔から**外来**の文化を取り入れつつ**自国なり**の文化をつくり上げるのが上手で、戦後の発展もそうした民族性に支えられてきました。

　しかし、高度経済成長期の東京への一極集中化と、それに準じた地方の急速な都市化がさまざまな**ひずみ**を招いています。例えば、地方都市の**没個性化**です。駅前の商店街はどこも同じような街並みに再開発され、住民が主体的に関わる伝統行事もめっきり少なくなりました。

　その反省から今、各地で地方発信の文化事業が計画、実行されています。その象徴がB級グルメで、あえて一流のA級としない点が地方の食文化の独自性を**際立たせ**ようとの試みと言えます。

□ 混在する　be mixed
□ 外来の　foreign
□ 〜なりの　in one's own way
□ ひずみ　strain
□ 没個性化　homogenizing
□ めっきり少なくなる　dwindle dramatically
□ 際立たせる　make something stand out

3 Modern-day Culture

Q: What are the features of Japanese culture today?

Present-day Japanese culture is a mixture of traditional culture and Western lifestyles. From the distant past the Japanese have been adept at adopting foreign influences and adapting them in a Japanese way. The postwar development of Japan owes its success to that trait.

However, the focus on Tokyo following the period of rapid economic development, as well as the urbanization of outlying areas, has produced certain stresses and strains in Japanese life. One of these is the homogenizing of provincial cities. The shopping areas in front of local train stations have been "developed" so that they all look the same, and the number of traditional events in which locals play an active role has dwindled dramatically.

In reaction to this, plans have been drawn up for promoting local cultures and are now being put into effect. One example of this is the promotion of so-called B-class cuisine, making the local specialties stand out by purposely not ranking them as A class.

第3章 文化

Q: 日本人はコメを食べなくなったの？

戦後の日本人が、欧米風の生活習慣を取り入れた最大のものが食文化です。1980年代後期には、家庭で主食としていたコメがパン・菓子類に取って代わられ、日本人のコメ離れが顕著になりました。この傾向はその後も続き、2013年には購入額で2～3倍もの差がついてしまっています(家計調査年報)。

❏ 世界文化遺産になった「和食」

2014年12月、ユネスコが「和食」を世界文化遺産に登録しました。ご飯に汁もの、おかず三種で構成された「和食」は、栄養バランスに優れた食事として評価されたのですが、"遺産"というのが気になります。

Q: コンビニはいくつあるの？

利便性が、現代の日本人の暮らしぶりの基本になっています。その一つの象徴がコンビニエンス・ストア、いわゆる「コンビニ」です。ここでは食料、飲料、本、文具などの日常必需品が数多く揃っているほか、公共料金の支払いや荷物を送ったりできます。24時間営業をしている店も多く、全国に5万店あります。最大規模のセブンイレブンは1万7177店、年間総売上3.78兆円です。(2015年1月現在)。

□ ～に取って代わられる be replaced by
□ 顕著に undeniable
□ 汁もの soup
□ 気になる be troubling
□ 暮らしぶり way of life
□ 揃っている lined up

Q: Is rice no longer eaten?

Postwar Western influence can be seen most clearly in the food Japanese now eat. Toward the end of the 1980s, what had until then been the staple food, rice, began to be replaced by bread and various confectionaries. The movement away from rice became an undeniable fact. By 2013 the purchase of bread etc. had become two to three times that of rice (Family Income and Expenditure Survey).

❏ Japanese Cuisine: An Intangible Cultural Heritage

In December 2014 UNESCO designated Japanese cuisine (*washoku*) an Intangible Cultural Heritage. The traditional Japanese meal consisting of a soup and three dishes was ranked highly for its nutritional value. However, the word "heritage" is troubling in that it seems to indicate something of merely historical interest.

松花堂弁当 Shokado bento

Q: How many convenience stores are there?

Convenience might be a byword of modern Japan, and its icon might be the convenience store (or *konbini* as it is familiarly known). There you can buy most of the items needed for everyday life, such as food, drink, books, stationary, and much more; you can also pay your utility bills and post packages for speedy delivery. Most of the 50,000 stores located nationwide are open 24/7. The largest chain, Seven-Eleven, has 17,177 stores and annual sales of ¥3.78 trillion (January 2015).

第3章 文化

今やコンビニは日本の**文化現象**とも言われますが、**小売店**がコンビニに取って代わられることにより地方都市の没個性化を促進している一面も指摘されています。

Q: スマホって、なに？

スマホとは、スマートフォンの短縮語です。コンビニと同様に近年の文化現象として特筆されるのが、「ケータイ」(携帯端末)です。音声による通信機能のみならず、メッセージの送信、情報収集、撮影、ゲーム、ショッピングなど、携帯とオンラインサイトは日本人に新たなライフスタイルと文化を**もたらし**ています。

スマホのサービスの一つがライン(LINE)で、24時間、無料で通話ができ、メール、写真、動画、音声を送ることもできます。そのため、**若い世代**がこれを利用することが多く、(しばしば中毒といえるほど依存する)日常的なネットワークツールになっています。しかし、ラインというバーチャル世界での**つながり**は**もろく**、依存症やいじめの原因になっているとして、未成年者の利用制限を求める意見も多いのです。

□ 文化現象 cultural phenomenon
□ 小売店 retailer
□ もたらす offer
□ 若い世代 young generation
□ つながり connection
□ もろい tenuous

Convenience stores can be viewed as a positive symbol of the pace of life today, but it is also true that they have forced many small, regional retailers out of business, contributing to the homogenization of local areas.

Q: What is a *sumaho*?

Sumaho is an abbreviation for smartphone. In addition to the convenience store, the mobile or cell phone has become a symbol of modern life, and the smartphone stands at the apex of that phenomenon. Needless to say, with a smartphone you can not only communicate with people by the spoken word but also send messages, collect data, take pictures, play games, shop, etc. It is the ultimate in convenience.

One of the services available on a smartphone in Japan (and elsewhere as well) is called Line. Line allows the user to exchange texts, images, video and audio, and conduct free VoIP conversations and video conferences. It is a free service available 24 hours a day. Line has many followers among young people (often to the extent of addiction), who like its ability to create networks of friends. On the con side, the connection between such virtual friends is often very tenuous and can lead to bullying. This has led to calls for restrictions on usage by young people.

第4章
レジャー

みなとみらい(神奈川県) Minatomirai, Kanagawa

Q: 日本人の余暇の過ごし方は？

『レジャー白書』(日本生産性本部)の余暇市場動向(2014年)によると、日本人が参加した余暇活動ベスト5は以下のとおりです。

```
1位   国内観光旅行   5590万人
2位   ドライブ       4690万人
3位   外食(余暇中)   4470万人
4位   読書           4440万人
5位   映画(映画館)   3780万人
```

その他、ショッピング、カラオケ、ウォーキングなどがベスト10内にランクされています。また、遊園地・テーマパークの入園者(2100万人)も増加傾向にあります。

□ 余暇 free time 　　□ ランクする rank
□ 白書 white paper 　□ 入園者 park visitor

Chapter 4
Leisure

Q: How do Japanese spend their free time?

According to the white paper produced by the Japan Productivity Center (2014), the top five ways Japanese spend their free time are as follows (number of people in parentheses):

1. Tourism within Japan   (55.9 million)
2. Driving   (46.9 million)
3. Eating out (during leisure time) (44.7 million)
4. Reading   (44.4 million)
5. Movies at theaters   (37.8 million)

In the top ten we also find shopping, karaoke, and walking. The number of people visiting amusement and theme parks is also on the rise (21 million).

第4章 レジャー

近年の余暇活動の傾向としては、**お金がかかる**ものは**敬遠する**人が増えています。また、**満足度**は10〜40代は低く、50代から上昇して70代は最高という結果が出ています。

Q: 海外旅行で人気がある国は？

日本人は年間約1000万人以上が、海外旅行をしています。人気が高いのはアジアでは韓国、台湾、香港、タイ、ベトナムなど、欧米ではハワイ、グアム、フランス、イタリアなどです。

Q: 日本独特のレジャー施設は？

外国人が驚くのは、パチンコ店とカラオケボックスの多さです。この2つは、日本で生まれて発展したレジャー施設の雄と言ってもよいでしょう。その他、日本独特のレジャー施設として健康ランドやスーパー銭湯などの温浴施設があります。また、公営ギャンブル施設としての競輪場、競艇場、オートレース場も日本だけに存在します。

□ お金がかかる　expensive
□ 敬遠する　avoid
□ 満足度　amount of satisfaction
□ 年間　annual
□ 雄　leader of a group

The recent trend is to avoid expensive activities. As for the amount of satisfaction gained from free-time activities, the lowest level is recorded for those aged from 10 to 40 and the highest for those of 50 or older, peaking at 70.

Q: What are the most popular destinations for foreign travel?

Some 10 million Japanese travel abroad every year. The most frequented Asian countries are South Korea, Taiwan, Hong Kong, Thailand, and Vietnam. The Western destinations most visited are Hawaii, Guam, France, and Italy.

Q: Are there any uniquely Japanese leisure facilities?

What often comes as a surprise to visitors to Japan is the huge number of karaoke boxes and pachinko pinball parlors. These two leisurely activities—Japan born and raised—stand head and shoulders above the rest. Other facilities characteristically Japanese include health spas, super hot springs, and other multipurpose therapeutic centers. There are also forms of legal gambling, such as cycling, boating, and motorcycle racing, that are only found in Japan.

Q: ゲームや漫画に熱中する大人がいるって、ほんとう？

日本では、ゲームや漫画は子ども達だけの楽しみではありません。20代、30代まで幅広い層に楽しまれています。例えば、週刊漫画雑誌は数百万部発行され、単行本になるとシリーズで数千万部発行される作品も少なくありません。ゲームは従来はテレビゲームが主流でしたが、近年は携帯端末でできるゲームの支持者が増加しています。電車の車内で、下を向いてゲームをしている若者の姿を見かけることも多いはずです。

☐ おたく

漫画（アニメ）やゲームの愛好者のなかでも際だって嗜好性が強い人の蔑称。1970年代に生まれた言葉で、電気街で知られる秋葉原（東京）は「おたく族のメッカ」とも呼ばれています。

☐ 熱中する　become enthusiastic
☐ 幅広い層　wide range of people
☐ 従来は　originally
☐ 支持者　follower
☐ 際だって　extraordinarily
☐ 蔑称　disparaging word

Q: Is it true that mature adults are just as enthusiastic about comics and video games as young people?

In Japan, comics (manga) and video games are not the exclusive province of the young. There is also a wide following among people in their twenties and thirties. An indication of this fact is that manga weekly magazines often have print-runs in the several hundreds of thousands, and when a manga comes out in serialized book form, it may sell several million copies. Video games were originally made to be played on a TV monitor but now the mobile phone is becoming the device of choice. In the trains you will notice a good number of young heads bent over their mobile phones.

❑ Otaku

Otaku refers to someone who takes his or her liking for anime, manga or video games to extraordinary lengths. The word emerged in the 1970s when the Akihabara district, known for its plethora of electronic and other geeky goods, came to be called the *Otaku* Mecca.

フィギュア
Character figures

秋葉原(東京都)
Akihabara, Tokyo

コスプレ
Cosplay

第4章 レジャー

Q: カラオケはいつからブームになったの？

　カラオケは「空」と「オーケストラ」を合体した略語です。「空」はリードヴォーカルのトラック部分がないことを意味しています。カラオケ機器の原型は、1970年代初期に登場しました。主流は、ビルのフロアを細かく仕切り個室にして時間貸しで楽しめるカラオケボックスで、全国に約9300施設あるとされます(カラオケ白書2014)。
　機器の多機能化も進み、音声変換や歌の採点などもできるようになっています。家庭向けのカラオケ内蔵マイクも普及していますが、他人の前で歌うところにこそカラオケの楽しさがあるのです。

Q: パチンコはどんな遊技なの？

　ピンボールと似たゲームで、多くの釘が打たれた盤面上に鋼球を打上げ、それが落下して特定の入賞口に入ると賞球が得られる遊技です。賞球は景品と交換できます。パチンコ店が登場したのは1930年代ですが、戦時中は全面禁止され、戦後に復活しました。70年代後半頃までは鋼球を手動で打っていましたが、その後は自動式になり、射出は0.6秒に1発以内と制限されています。
　現在のパチンコ台は、アニメなどの作品を題材とした「タイアップ機」が主流で、入賞時に興奮させたり大当たりの期待感を高めるさまざまな機能を備えています。景品の換金も行われているため、射幸心をあおるギャンブル要素が強いと指摘され、パチンコ依存症が社会問題になっています。

□ 合体する　combine
□ 登場する　appear
□ 主流　usual style
□ 時間貸し　pay-by-the-hour
□ 全面禁止　blanket ban
□ 射出　fire

Q: When did karaoke begin to boom?

The word karaoke combines the Japanese word for empty with a shortened version of orchestra. "Empty" refers to the fact that the track for the lead vocal is empty. The first karaoke device appeared at the beginning of the 1970s. The usual arrangement is for one floor of a building to be divided up into many small karaoke boxes for rent. There are said to be some 9,300 such facilities nationwide (Karaoke White Paper).

The karaoke device has become more sophisticated over time, with the addition of voice distortion and even the awarding of points for performance. Home karaoke devices with a built-in microphone are also available, but the ultimate pleasure of karaoke is still singing before an audience.

Q: What is pachinko?

Pachinko refers to a pinball-like game in which a ball is shot onto a vertical board, falls through many pins, and produces extra balls when the launched ball falls into the appropriate slots. These newly won balls can be exchanged for prizes. The first pachinko parlors appeared in the 1930s, only to be banned during the war and then reappear in the postwar period. The balls were released manually until near the end of the 1970s, when automatic firing came into use, with the restriction that a shot could only be fired every 0.6 seconds.

The majority of pachinko machines today are video-oriented with tie-ups to anime creators and other visual artists. They have a good many features that heighten the moment, or the expectation, of winning a jackpot. Since the prizes can be exchanged for money, pachinko is actually an addictive form of gambling, and for that reason its social value has been questioned.

☐ 期待感を高める heighten the expectation
☐ 射幸心をあおる arouse the passion for jackpot

パチンコ
Pachinko

第5章
観光・イベント

伏見稲荷大社(京都府) Fushimi inari-taisha shrine, Kyoto

1 観光

Q: 日本への観光客が多い国は？

　来日する外国人は年間約1340万人で、その8割がアジアの国々からの来客です。ベスト3は、台湾(約283万人)、韓国(約275万人)、中国(約241万人)。

　中国人観光客が多いのが春節の大型連休がある2月で、日本の観光地は中国人の観光ツアーで混雑します。近年、観光客が急増しているのがタイで、65万人強(前年比伸び率45％)。タイでは、4月の連休を利用した訪日ツアーが流行しています。(数値は2014年、日本政府観光局調べ)。日本政府は、2020年の東京五輪までに年間2000万人を目標にしています。

□ 来日する　come to Japan
□ 来客　guest
□ 観光ツアー　tour group
□ 伸び率　growth rate
□ 連休を利用する　take advantage of consecutive holidays

Chapter 5
Tourism and Special Events

1 Tourism

Q: What countries send the most visitors to Japan?

The number of tourists coming to Japan every year is about 13.4 million, of which 80% are from Asia. The top three are Taiwan (about 2.83 million), South Korea (about 2.75 million), and China (about 2.41 million).

Chinese tourists are particularly prominent in February during the Chinese Spring Festival, when there are a number of consecutive holidays. During this time the Japanese tourist attractions are crowded with Chinese tour groups. Thailand, on the other hand, has shown remarkable increases in recent years (over 650,000; up more than 45% over the previous year), taking advantage of consecutive holidays in April. The government has set a goal of 20,000,000 annual visitors by the 2020 Tokyo Olympics.

第5章　観光・イベント

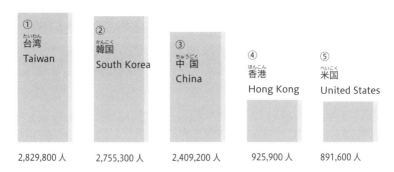

● 訪日観光客が多い国・地域ベスト10（2014年1月〜12月）

① 台湾 Taiwan　2,829,800人
② 韓国 South Korea　2,755,300人
③ 中国 China　2,409,200人
④ 香港 Hong Kong　925,900人
⑤ 米国 United States　891,600人

Q: 外国人に人気がある観光地は？

外国人観光客が集中するのは、東京、京都、大阪の3都市で約8割と言われます。最も人気があるのが京都で、ついでに奈良を巡る古都観光です。京都では伏見稲荷大社、金閣寺、清水寺、祇園などが人気スポット。東京ではスカイツリーや浅草寺などの下町を巡るバスツアーを楽しむ観光客が多く、新宿のゴールデン街や渋谷のスクランブル交差点も人気があります。

また近年、外国人観光客が増えているのが、日本の里山の原風景ともいえる白川郷（世界遺産、岐阜県）、平成の大修理を終えた国宝・姫路城（世界遺産、兵庫県）をはじめとする城巡りです。北陸新幹線の開業で行きやすくなった古都・金沢は今後、外国人観光客が増加すると見られています。

□ 集中する　concentrate
□ ついでに　use an opportunity to
□ 巡る　walk about
□ 原風景　landscape of the heart
□ 城巡り　castle tour
□ 開業　opening

● The top 10 countries and regions sending visitors to Japan are:
 (All figures provided by the Japan National Tourist Organization, 2014.)

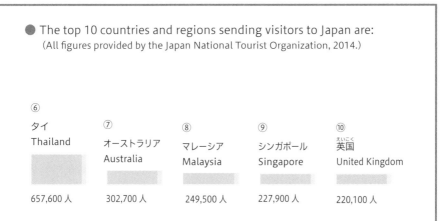

⑥ タイ Thailand	⑦ オーストラリア Australia	⑧ マレーシア Malaysia	⑨ シンガポール Singapore	⑩ 英国 United Kingdom
657,600 人	302,700 人	249,500 人	227,900 人	220,100 人

Q: What are the most popular tourist sites?

Approximately 80% of visitors to Japan concentrate their time in the three big cities of Tokyo, Kyoto, and Osaka. Kyoto is the most popular, with many people making a side trip to nearby Nara. Kyoto is especially noted for Fushimi Inari Shrine, Kinkaku-ji (Golden Pavilion), Kiyomizu-dera temple, and the Gion district. In Tokyo, many visitors take the bus tour to the Skytree tower, Senso-ji temple, and the surrounding area that preserves the plebeian atmosphere of old Tokyo. The cramped Shinjuku Golden Gai area, famous for its architectural interest and nightlife, and the Shibuya scramble crossing are also attractions.

Of late, visitors hoping to get a taste of "good old" Japan have increasingly visited Shirakawa-go, an old farming village with a distinctive type of architecture in Gifu prefecture (World Heritage Site), and the recently renovated Himeji Castle in Hyogo prefecture (World Heritage Site), among other castles. With the new Hokuriku Shinkansen now in operation, the well-preserved historical town of Kanazawa can be easily reached from Tokyo and will surely become a favorite tourist destination.

白川郷(岐阜県)
Shirakawa-go, Gifu

Q: 宿泊施設にはどんなものがあるの？

日本の観光客向け宿泊施設は、旅館と観光ホテルに大別されます。旅館は純日本式、温泉地に多い観光ホテルは和洋ミックスです。「政府登録」の旅館やホテルがありますが、これは政府が定める**基準を満たした施設**ということで、ステイタスではありません。日本では欧米のようなホテルの**公的格付け**がないため、料金を基準に施設を選ぶ必要があります。

Q: 世界遺産に登録されているのは、どこ？

ユネスコが、**自然のままの**地や歴史的建造物・遺跡などを指定して「世界遺産リスト」に登録した件数は1007件（2014年12月現在）。日本の「世界遺産」は、以下のとおりです。

自然遺産

❶ 白神山地
　（青森県・秋田県、1993年12月登録）

❷ 屋久島
　（鹿児島県、1993年12月）

❸ 知床
　（北海道、2005年7月）

❹ 小笠原諸島
　（東京都、2011年6月）

□ 〜向け　aimed at
□ 基準を満たす　meet a standard
□ 公的格付け　official grading
□ 〜を基準に　base on
□ 自然のまま　unspoiled

Q: What kinds of accommodations are there for tourists?

Accommodations for foreign visitors can be broadly divided into tourist hotels and Japanese inns. Inns are purely Japanese in their arrangements and layout, while the tourist hotels found near hot springs are a mixture of Japanese and Western fixtures. Some inns and hotels are "officially registered" by the government, but since Japan does not have hotel rankings like in the West, this simply means that the hotel or inn has met basic government standards. In the end, you must choose based on price and your own taste.

Q: How many World Heritage Sites are there?

World Heritage Site is a building, city, complex, desert, forest, island, lake, monument, or mountain that is listed by UNESCO as being of special cultural or physical significance. As of December 2014, there are 1,007 such sites. The Japanese sites are as follows:

Natural Sites

❶ Shirakami-Sanchi
(Aomori and Akita prefectures; listed December 1993)

❷ Yakushima
(Kagoshima prefecture; listed December 1993)

❸ Shiretoko
(Hokkaido prefecture; listed July 2005)

❹ Ogasawara Islands
(Tokyo Metropolis; listed June 2011)

文化遺産

① 姫路城
　（兵庫県、1993年12月登録）
② 法隆寺地域の仏像建造物
　（奈良県、1993年12月）
③ 古都京都の文化財
　（京都府・滋賀、1994年12月）
④ 白川郷・五箇山の合掌造り集落
　（岐阜県・富山県、1995年12月）
⑤ 厳島神社
　（広島県、1996年12月）
⑥ 原爆ドーム
　（広島県、1996年12月）
⑦ 古都奈良の文化財
　（奈良県、1998年12月）
⑧ 日光の社寺
　（栃木県、1999年12月）
⑨ 琉球王国のグスク及び関連遺産群
　（沖縄県、2000年12月）
⑩ 紀伊山地の霊場と参詣道
　（三重県・奈良県・和歌山県、2004年7月）
⑪ 石見銀山遺跡とその文化的景観
　（島根県、2007年7月）
⑫ 平泉――仏国土（浄土）を表す建築・庭園及び考古学的遺跡群
　（岩手県、2011年6月）
⑬ 富士山――信仰の対象と芸術の源泉
　（静岡県・山梨県、2013年6月）
⑭ 富岡製糸場と絹産業遺跡群
　（群馬県、2014年6月）

姫路城（兵庫県）
Himeji-jo castle, Hyogo

厳島神社（広島県）
Itsukushima shinto shrine, Hiroshima

Cultural Sites

① Himeji-jo
(Hyogo prefecture; listed December 1993)

② Buddhist Monuments in the Horyu-ji Area
(Nara prefecture; December 1993)

③ Historic Monuments of Ancient Kyoto
(Kyoto and Shiga prefectures; listed December 1994)

④ Historic Villages of Shirakawa-go and Gokayama
(Gifu and Toyama prefectures; listed December 1995)

⑤ Itsukushima Shinto Shrine
(Hiroshima prefecture; listed December 1996)

⑥ Hiroshima Peace Memorial
(Genbaku Dome, Hiroshima prefecture; listed December 1996)

⑦ Historic Monuments of Ancient Nara
(Nara prefecture; listed December 1998)

⑧ Shrines and Temples of Nikko
(Tochigi prefecture; listed December 1999)

⑨ Gusuku Sites and Related Properties of the Kingdom of Ryukyu
(Okinawa prefecture; listed December 2000)

⑩ Sacred Sites and Pilgrimage Routes in the Kii Mountain Range
(Mie, Nara, Wakayama prefectures; listed July 2004)

⑪ Iwami Ginzan Silver Mine and its Cultural Landscape
(Shimane prefecture; listed July 2007)

⑫ Hiraizumi—Temples, Gardens and Archaeological Sites Representing the Buddhist Pure Land
(Iwate prefecture; listed June 2011)

⑬ Fujisan, sacred place and source of artistic inspiration
(Shizuoka and Yamanashi prefectures; listed June 2013)

⑭ Tomioka Silk Mill and Related Sites
(Gunma prefecture; listed June 2014)

清水寺（京都府）
Kiyomizu temple, Kyoto

富岡製糸場（群馬県）
Tomioka silk mill, Gunma

第5章 観光・イベント

なお、明治日本の産業革命遺産（福岡県など8県）を文化遺産として登録勧告中（2015年5月現在）。

Q: 温泉って、なに？

火山列島の日本には、地下にたくさんの温泉・鉱泉が存在します。摂氏25度以上が温泉で、それ未満を鉱泉と言います。

温泉施設は2万以上もあるとされますが、天然温泉はその3割ほどで、有名な温泉地でも施設が増えたことで源泉から供給される湯量が不足ぎみになり、水増し湯や循環湯でカバーしているケースが目立ちます。湯船からあふれたお湯を流しっぱなしの「源泉かけ流し」かどうかが、適正な天然温泉かそうでないかを見分けるポイントです。

Q: 有名な温泉地は、どこ？

数多い温泉地の中から選ぶのは難しいのですが、温泉ランキングなどを参考にすると、以下の温泉地が挙げられます。

□ 勧告　recommendation
□ 鉱泉　mineral water
□ 摂氏　Celsius
□ 不足ぎみ　in short supply
□ 〜のケースが目立つ　often happen to see
□ 流しっぱなし　allow to run freely
□ 源泉かけ流し　natural hot spring water from the original source continually overflowing
□ 見分ける　recognize

Further, eight sites in Fukuoka prefecture and elsewhere that are connected with industrial development in the Meiji period (1868-1912) are now on the Tentative List (as of May 2015).

Q: What distinguishes Japanese hot springs?

Japan being a volcanic archipelago, it has many hot springs and mineral water sites. Water above 25 degrees Celsius is considered a hot spring; below that, it is mineral water.

There are said to be over 20,000 hot spring resorts nationwide, but only one-third of them use natural hot spring water. The number of resorts has grown to such an extent that even in the most famous hot spring areas, there is a lamentable shortage of natural thermal water, meaning that it has to be augmented from other sources or recycled. You can tell if the water is from a natural hot spring by whether it is allowed to run freely out of the bathing area.

Q: Which hot spring areas are the most well-known?

While it is difficult to come up with an impartial list, a comparison of various listings and rankings produces the following.

草津温泉・湯畑 (群馬県)
Yubatake (Kusatsu onsen), Gunma

東日本

登別（北海道）
秋保（宮城県）
那須・鬼怒川（栃木県）
草津・伊香保（群馬県）
強羅・箱根（神奈川県）
熱海・湯河原・伊東（静岡県）など。

温泉旅館の風呂（強羅温泉、神奈川県）
Onsen ryokan's bath (Gora onsen), Kanagawa

西日本

下呂（岐阜県）
有馬・城崎（兵庫県）
白浜（和歌山県）
山中（石川県）
玉造（島根県）
道後（愛媛県）
黒川（熊本県）
別府・湯布院（大分県）
指宿（鹿児島県）など。

道後温泉（愛媛県）
Dogo onsen, Ehime

❏ 熱海温泉

1200年以上の歴史を持つ日本有数の温泉地。東京から新幹線で35〜50分、車で約2時間という至便性から観光客が多く、60軒以上のホテルや旅館があります。夏と冬は花火大会が開催されます。

□ 日本有数の one of Japan's most famous　　　□ 至便性 convenience

Eastern Japan

- Noboribetsu (Hokkaido)
- Akiu (Miyagi prefecture)
- Nasu and Kinugawa (Tochigi prefecture)
- Kusatsu and Ikaho (Gunma prefecture)
- Gora and Hakone (Kanagawa prefecture)
- Atami, Yugawara, and Ito (Shizuoka prefecture)

Western Japan

- Gero (Gifu prefecture)
- Arima and Kinosaki (Hyogo prefecture)
- Shirahama (Wakayama prefecture)
- Yamanaka (Ishikawa prefecture)
- Tamatsukuri (Shimane prefecture)
- Dogo (Ehime prefecture)
- Kurokawa (Kumamoto prefecture)
- Beppu and Yufuin (Oita prefecture)
- Ibusuki (Kagoshima prefecture)

城崎温泉（兵庫県）
Kinosaki onsen, Hyogo

❏ Atami Hot Springs

With a history of over 1,200 years, Atami is one of Japan's most famous hot spring resorts. It can be conveniently reached from Tokyo by shinkansen in 35 to 55 minutes, or by car in about 2 hours, accounting in part for its many visitors. It boasts over 60 hotels and inns. There is a magnificent fireworks display in both summer and winter.

熱海（静岡県）
Atami, Shizuoka

Q: 日本のおみやげで人気があるのは？

　円安や東南アジア、中国向けのビザ緩和を追い風に、訪日外国人客数が急増しています。外国人旅行者を対象に消費税抜きで商品を販売できる免税店も増加し、1万8000店になりました（2015年5月）。2014年10月には、家電・バッグ・衣料品などに加え、食料品・医薬品・化粧品も対象にされました。

　ちなみに、中国人観光客は医薬品・化粧品・家電・バッグなどを"爆買い"することで話題になっていますが、意外な人気商品は温水洗浄便座だそうです。

　東京でのおみやげを買う場所としては、浅草仲見世、秋葉原電気街、上野アメ横商店街などが主で、それぞれ日本人形、電気炊飯器、タラバガニが人気商品です。

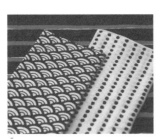

手ぬぐい
Tenugui, Japanese hand towel

市松人形
Ichimatsu dolls

- □ 〜を追い風に　thanks to
- □ 急増する　increase dramatically
- □ 爆買い　splurge buying
- □ 話題になる　much-talked-about
- □ 意外な　unexpected
- □ 便座　toilet seat

Q What are the most popular souvenirs?

What with the appreciation of the yen and the loosening of tourist visa restrictions for Southeast Asia and China, the number of tourists coming to Japan has shown a dramatic increase. The number of tax-free shops where tourists can make purchases without paying the consumer tax has also grown to 18,000 shops (as of May 2015). In October 2014, in addition to electric appliances, handbags, and clothing, foodstuffs, pharmaceuticals, and cosmetics were also added to the list of tax-free items.

A much-talked-about recent event is the splurge buying of pharmaceuticals, cosmetics, electric appliances, and handbags by tourists from China, among which items is the popular toilet seat that both heats the posterior and washes it with water.

The principal places to buy souvenirs in Tokyo are Asakusa's Nakamise, Akihabara's Electric Town, and Ueno's Ameya Yokocho, where you can buy things like Japanese dolls, electric rice cookers, red king crab, and a multitude of other items.

浅草仲見世(東京都)
Asakusa's Nakamise, Tokyo

Q: 国宝って、どのように決めるの？

国宝は、**文字どおり**日本の「国の宝」です。国が指定した重要文化財のなかで特に世界文化の**見地から**価値の高いものが選ばれ、文部科学大臣が指定します。2014年現在、国宝の指定件数は以下のとおりです。

建造物221件、絵画159件、彫刻128件、工芸品252件、書跡・典籍224件、古文書60件、考古資料46件、歴史資料3件。

国宝を多く収蔵して展示しているのが国立博物館で、東京・京都・奈良・九州(福岡県)の4館があります。なかでも東京国立博物館(上野)は収蔵件数が多く、常設展示も行っています。

□ 文字通り literally
□ 〜の見地から in terms of
□ 価値の高い high-value
□ 収蔵する house

Q: How is a National Treasure designated?

The Japanese word for National Treasure (*kokuho*) literally means "treasure of the nation." National Treasures are chosen from a list of Important Cultural Properties for their high value in terms of world cultural history, and are designated by the Minister of Education, Culture, Sports, Science and Technology. As of 2014, the number of National Treasures was as follows: buildings, 221; paintings, 159; sculpture, 128; crafts, 252; written materials, 224; ancient documents, 60; archaeological artifacts, 46; historical artifacts, 3.

Many of these National Treasures are housed in the national museums in Tokyo, Kyoto, Nara, and Kyushu (Fukuoka). The Tokyo National Museum in Ueno has an exceptionally large number of National Treasures, many of which are on permanent display.

東京 国立博物館
Tokyo National Museum

第5章 観光・イベント

Q: 仏像にはどんな種類があるの？

仏像は、仏教での信仰の対象としてつくられました。中国や韓国から渡来した像をもとに日本の仏師が独自に制作するようになったのは奈良時代前後で、平安時代や鎌倉時代には芸術的に優れた仏像が生み出されました。

仏像は、①如来像、②菩薩像、③明王像、④天部像の4種に大別されます。如来像は仏の姿を現したもので、仏教の世界観では釈迦だけでなく、たくさんの仏がいるとしています。菩薩像は仏になるための修行中の姿、明王像は悪魔から仏を守る神々、天部像はインドのバラモンの神々を表現しています。

❑ 大仏

日本には「大仏」と呼ばれる仏像が90ほどあり、なかでも高さ10m以上の像は30ほどです。奈良・東大寺の大仏は749年完成で金銅の仏像として世界最大（高さ約16m）、鎌倉・長谷寺の大仏は13世紀中頃の造立、台座を含め高さ約13.3mです。

□ 信仰の対象　religious object
□ 仏師　sculptor of Buddhist statues
□ 現す　show
□ 世界観　world view
□ 造立　set up

Q: What kinds of Buddhist sculpture are there?

Buddhist statues were created as religious objects of worship. Buddhist sculpture first came to Japan from China and Korea, and working with these statues as models, Japanese sculptors began to add their own individual styles around the beginning of the Nara period (710-784). By the Heian period (784-1185) and Kamakura period (1185-1333) works of outstanding artistic merit were being created.

Buddhist statues can be broadly classified by the figure they depict: 1) Nyorai, 2) Bosatsu, 3) Myoo, and 4) Tenbu. Nyorai refers to those who have attained enlightenment or become a Buddha, not simply to the historical Buddha, Shakamuni. Bosatsu, or Bodhisattva, refers to a figure who is still undergoing ascetic practices to become a Buddha. Myoo refers to deities who protect Buddhas from devils. Tenbu refers to gods incorporated from Indian Brahmanism.

❏ Great Buddha Statues

There are 90 statues that are classified as Great Buddhas, or Daibutsu. Of these, 30 are over 10 meters in height. The Great Buddha at Todai-ji in Nara, completed in 749, is the world's largest bronze statue of Dainichi Nyorai (Vairocana) at 16 meters. The Great Buddha at Hasedera in Kamakura, completed in mid 13th century, is 13.3 meters tall, including the base.

鎌倉の大仏（神奈川県）
Great Buddha of Kamakura, Kanagawa

Q: お城は、いくつあるの？

記録に残っている城は2万5000もあったとされますが、**現存**する城跡はその1％にも**足り**ません。日本の城と言えば天守閣のある城が好まれますが、観光名所としての城は60ほどで**復元・復興**したものも含まれます。

国宝に指定されている城は、姫路城（世界遺産、兵庫県）、松本城（長野県）、彦根城（滋賀県）、犬山城（愛知県）、松江城（島根県）です。

2　イベント

Q: 有名な祭りは？

一般的に「日本の三大祭」と呼ばれているのが、神田祭（東京・神田明神、5月**中旬**）、天神祭（大阪・天満宮、6月**下旬**～7月25日）、祇園祭（京都・八坂神社、7月1ヵ月間）です。

その他、全国からたくさんの観光客が訪れる祭りとして有名なのが、よさこい祭り（8月9日～12日、高知県高知市、100万人）、青森ねぶた祭（8月2日～7日、青森県青森市、250万人）、さっぽろ雪まつり（2月5日～11日、北海道札幌市、240万人）などです。（会期・集客数は2014年のデータ）

- □ 現存する　survive
- □ 足りない　less
- □ 復元　rebuilding
- □ 復興　reconstruction
- □ 中旬　mid
- □ 下旬　late

Q: How many castles are there?

According to historical records, there were once as many as 25,000, but now less than 1% survive in one form or another. Among the 60 castles most frequented by tourists are many that have undergone rebuilding or reconstruction.

The castles listed as National Treasures are as follows: Himeji (World Heritage Site; Hyogo prefecture), Matsumoto (Nagano prefecture), Hikone (Shiga prefecture), Inuyama (Aichi prefecture), and Matsue (Shimane prefecture).

2 Special Events

Q: What are the most famous festivals?

The three known as the Three Great Festivals of Japan are the Kanda Festival (Tokyo: Kanda Myojin shrine, mid May), Tenjin Festival (Osaka: Tenman-gu shrine, from late June to late July), and Gion Festival (Kyoto: Yasaka shrine, July).

Other famous festivals that attract people from around the country (with number of attendants in parentheses) are: Yosakoi Festival (Kochi city, Kochi prefecture: August 9-12, 1 million), Aomori Nebuta Festival (Aomori city, Aomori prefecture: August 2-7, 2.5 million), and the Sapporo Snow Festival (Sapporo city, Hokkaido: February 5-11, 2.4 million). (Dates and statistics based on 2014 data.)

祇園祭（京都府）
Gion festival, Kyoto

Q: 祭りは、なんのためにやるの？

　古くからの神事が、その由来です。日本人は**豊作**や**豊漁**を願って年1回、神社に祀られている神様の**威光が増す**ようにと神輿に乗せて外へ連れ出しました。これが祭りに発展したのです。また、祭りは神道でのハレ（非日常性）の儀式で、日常生活を離れた世界で身を浄めるという**意味合い**もあります。

　奇祭と言われるものも多くあります。例えば、西宮神社福男選び（兵庫県、1月）は、多くの男女が神社の**境内**を200メートルほど競争し、その年の福男を決めます。西大寺はだか祭（岡山県、2月）では、**まわし姿**の男たちがその年の福男を競います。宇出津あばれ（石川県、7月）は、松明や神輿が水中や火中に投げ込まれる**勇壮な**祭りです。一方、笑い祭り（和歌山県、10月）は、道化に**扮した**人が人々に笑うように言いながら練り歩くというもの。新年の行事である男鹿のなまはげ（秋田県、大晦日）は、恐ろしい鬼の面をかぶった人が家を訪ね、怖がる子供にいい子になるようにと言います。岸和田だんじり祭（大阪府、9月）では、大きな神輿が町を**疾走する**という危険なもので、7年に1度開催される諏訪大社の御柱祭（長野県）は、人を乗せたままの大木を急な坂から落とすため、死傷者が出ることでも知られます。

- □ 豊作　bountiful harvest
- □ 豊漁　plentiful fishi
- □ 威光が増す　increase prestige
- □ 意味合い　overtone
- □ 境内　shrine compound
- □ 福男　lucky man
- □ まわし姿の　loinclothed
- □ 勇壮な　brave
- □ 扮する　disguise
- □ 疾走する　careen

Q: What is the purpose of a festival?

The origin of the festival (*matsuri*) is found in Shinto religious rites stemming from the distant past. Once a year, in the hope of having a bountiful harvest and plentiful fishing, shrine parishioners would take the god out of the shrine in a sacred palanquin to spread the god's blessings far and wide. This custom eventually developed into the festivals we see today. This coincides with the Shinto notion of *hare* ("bright") rituals, which mark a time when participants are transported to a world of the extraordinary and purify themselves of the dross of everyday life.

Some of these festivals are termed "bizarre" (*kisai*). For instance, there is a race held as part of a festival at Nishinomiya Shrine (Hyogo prefecture, January), in which crowds of men (and women) sprint over 200 meters through the shrine compound to see who wins and is named the lucky man of the year. There is also the Naked Festival at Saidai-ji temple (Okayama prefecture, February), where loinclothed men compete for the "lucky man" honor. At Ushitsu on the Noto Peninsula (Ishikawa prefecture, July), there is an *abare* (violent) festival featuring bonfires, fiery lanterns, sacred palanquins being thrown into the sea, retrieved and then incinerated. On the other hand, there is the Laughing Festival (Wakayama prefecture, October), in which clown-like parishioners parade the streets, encouraging everyone to laugh and laughing themselves. In a New Year's ritual in Akita prefecture, men dressed as ogres (*namahage*) and wearing large, frightful masks go from house to house admonishing quaking children to be on good behavior. In the Kishiwada Danjiri Festival (Osaka, September), huge sacred palanquins careen dangerously through the streets, and in the Onbashira Festival in Nagano prefecture, held once every seven years, participants ride on huge logs shooting down a precipitous slope. Fatalities are not unheard of.

御柱祭 (長野県)
Onbashira festival, Nagano

Q: 花火大会は、いつから始まったの？

江戸時代の享保年間(1716-35)に疫病が流行し、犠牲者の供養と悪疫払いのために大川での水神祭で20発打ち上げたのが始まり。当時は和火といって、色数も少なく地味な花火でした。競技花火大会がはじまり、なかでも大曲の全国花火競技大会(秋田県)、土浦全国花火競技大会(茨城県)、長岡まつり大花火大会(新潟県)は有名です。

❑ 東京 "三大" 花火大会

最も古い歴史がある「隅田川花火大会」(7月最終土曜日)は約2万発、見物客90万人。「江戸川区花火大会」(8月第1土曜日)は約1万2000発、140万人。ベイエリアでの「東京湾大華火祭」(8月第2土曜日)は約1万2000発、70万人。

Q: 灯篭流しって、なに？

「灯篭流し」は、お盆に死者の霊をなぐさめるために、木や竹の枠に和紙をはった灯篭の中のろうそくに火をともして川や海へ流す風習です。お供え物や花を一緒に流すケースもありますが、汚染につながるとして禁止する自治体もあり、昔ほど一般的ではなくなりました。

☐ 疫病 epidemic
☐ 悪疫払い purifying ritual
☐ 地味な subdued
☐ 死者の霊 spirit of the dead
☐ 汚染につながる contribute to pollution

Q: When did fireworks displays first begin?

In the Kyoho era (1716-35) of the Edo period, an epidemic broke out, and 20 fireworks were shot off to console the spirits of the dead. The number of colors was small, and the overall effect was rather subdued. Later, competitive fireworks displays came into being, the most famous being the Omagari National Japan Fireworks Competition (Akita prefecture), the Tsuchiura All Japan Fireworks Competition (Ibaraki prefecture), and the Nagaoka Festival Fireworks (Niigata prefecture).

❏ Tokyo's Three Great Fireworks Displays

The oldest of the three is the Sumidagawa Fireworks Festival (last Saturday of July), where some 20,000 fireworks are shot off before 900,000 people. Then there is the Edogawa Ward Fireworks Festival (first Saturday in August) with 12,000 fireworks before 1,400,000 people, and the Tokyo Bay Grand Fireworks Festival (second Saturday in August) with 12,000 fireworks launched before 700,000 people.

隅田川花火大会(東京都)
Sumidagawa fireworks festival, Tokyo

Q: What is lantern floating?

"Lantern floating" (*toro nagashi*) refers to the custom during Obon (Festival of the Dead) when lanterns made of wood or bamboo and covered with Japanese paper (*washi*), with a candle inside, are floated down streams or in the ocean as a means of consoling the dead. Sometimes flowers or other offerings are included, but deciding that this might contribute to pollution, some local governments have outlawed the practice, with the result that it is not as common as it used to be.

嵐山灯篭流し(京都府)
Arashiyama lantern floating, Kyoto

第5章 観光・イベント

ピースメッセージとうろう流し（広島市）は、原爆ドームの**対岸**の元安川で被爆者などの慰霊と世界平和へのメッセージを書いた約1万個の灯篭を流します。灯篭流しは花火大会と一緒に行われることが多く、京都嵐山灯篭流し花火大会（桂川）が有名です。九州の長崎市内陸部、佐賀市・熊本市の一部では「精霊流し」と呼び、船を使うこともあります。

Q: かまくらって、なに？

秋田県や新潟県などの雪国で、雪を**盛り固めて**つくった家（雪洞）の中に**祭壇を設けて**水神を祀る、小正月（2月中旬頃）の伝統行事です。みちのく（東北）五大雪まつりの一つの「横手かまくら」（秋田県横手市）は400年以上の歴史を持ち、雪まつり期間中は100基ほどのかまくらが登場し、その中に入った子ども達が甘酒やお餅を**振る舞い**ます。横手より古い歴史を持つ「六郷かまくら」（秋田県美郷町）は、国の重要無形文化財に指定され、2月11日〜15日の間、神事が行われます。最終日の竹うちは、住民男性が**2手に分かれ**5ｍの長竹で打ち合って吉凶を占う、**荒々しい**行事です。

□ 対岸　opposite shore
□ 盛り固める　pack
□ 祭壇を設ける　erect an altar
□ 振る舞う　treat
□ 2手に分かれる　divide into two groups
□ 荒々しい　rough

In Hiroshima city, there is the tradition of floating lanterns for peace on the Motoyasu river, across from the Atomic Dome, to console the spirits of those who died from the bomb there. Some 10,000 lanterns are released containing messages for world peace. Often lantern floating is combined with a fireworks display, one famous example being Kyoto's Arashiyama Lantern Floating Festival on the Katsura river. In the cities of Nagasaki, Saga, and Kumamoto this custom is called spirit floating (*shoro nagashi*) and includes boat-sized floats.

Q: What is a *kamakura*?

In often snow-laden Akita and Niigata prefectures, it is customary on the lunar New Year (mid February) to make igloo-like huts (*kamakura*) out of packed snow and erect therein altars to the gods of water. One of the Five Great Festivals of Michinoku (the Tohoku region), the Yokote Kamakura Festival (Yokote city, Akita prefecture) has a history of over 400 years. During the period of the festival, some 100 *kamakura* are built and occupied by children treating passersby to "sweet sake" (*amazake*) and rice cakes (*mochi*). Even older than the Yokote Kamakura Festival is the Rokugo Kamakura Event (Misato, Akita prefecture: February 11-15), which has been designated an Intangible Cultural Property. The last day of the event features the *take-uchi* ("bamboo-beating") competition, in which two teams of local men attack one another with 5-meter bamboo poles as a means of divining local prospects for the coming year.

横手かまくら（秋田県）
Yokote Kamakura, Akita

装　幀＝斉藤　啓（ブッダプロダクションズ）
本文イラスト＝テッド高橋
翻　訳＝Michael Brase

Furigana JAPAN
現代日本の暮らし Q&A
Everything You Should Know
about the Life of Modern Japan Q&A

2017年5月3日　第1刷発行

著　者　安部　直文
発行者　浦　晋亮
発行所　IBCパブリッシング株式会社
〒162-0804 東京都新宿区中里町29番3号　菱秀神楽坂ビル9F
Tel. 03-3513-4511　Fax. 03-3513-4512
www.ibcpub.co.jp

印刷所　中央精版印刷株式会社

© IBC Publishing, Inc. 2017

Printed in Japan

落丁本・乱丁本は、小社宛にお送りください。送料小社負担にてお取り替えいたします。
本書の無断複写（コピー）は著作権法上での例外を除き禁じられています。

ISBN978-4-7946-0478-1